The whole earth is the tomb of heroic men,
and their story is not craven only on stone over
their clay but abides everywhere, without visible
symbol, woven into the stuff of other men's lives.
Thucydides

By the same author:
Healing with Colour
The Pocket Book of Colour Power

colour
TALKS!

Discover the messages of your
true colours and make light
work of relationships

PHILIPPA MERIVALE

Laramar♥

Cover design and text illustrations by: Ben Cracknell Studios

ISBN: 1-903249-01-5

Printed in UK by Butler & Tanner Ltd

Laramar
Gloucestershire, UK.

CONTENTS

For John,
Nicola, Stephen and Magdalen,
in loving memory of
Roger and Anne

INTRODUCTION

Wh“hen we were children we thought as children: we believed in a
magical threshold which divided our experience from that of adults.
At some time in the future we would cross that threshold and –
abracadabra! – we would find ourselves on the other side, fully
equipped for life in the adult world. We would take with us our hopes and dreams,
and, with the power of our grown-up status, make them into reality. We would be
strong, confident and healthy; we would know what we wanted and how to
achieve it. Surrounded, in harmony and happiness, by those we loved, we would
offer our own unique contribution to those around us and make the world a
better place. With the clarity of childhood, we knew the power of our potential.
Yet, for many (or most) of us, time progressed and brought with it the frustrations
of daily life which, little by little, eroded our dreams. It may even have dawned
on us, at some point, that the magical threshold must have long since been
crossed; but where were those elusive tools and skills?

Have you ever felt like that? Have you ever wondered what happened to the
ideals and ambitions that dangled only just ahead of you, like a bunch of keys that
seemed a mere inch or two beyond your grasp, as you grew through adolescence
and early maturity? Have you wondered why the life you live now so often seems
to fall short of those early promises? Have you wondered "what if?....". What if
this job had been satisfying, you had made more money, moved to that house you
wanted? Have you wondered why the relationships in your life that started out

so joyful and wondrous peaked and troughed, and perhaps became a major challenge, sometimes being crushed but more often subsiding into a dull routine, or even into a miserable marriage?

What few people probably told you, through those years when you did your best to acquire some of the skills necessary for adult life, was that the most powerful tools were not ones that you would gain from outer teachers, qualifications and expertise, but those that already existed inside you, merely waiting to be discovered. The real power to unzip your potential and create what is best and most fulfilling for you and those you love is contained within that mysterious and potent entity which is your self. And the real obstacles to creating whatever it is that you want, believe in or need, are to be found in exactly the same place: within yourself, and in the limiting beliefs that you hold. Through years of conditioning, with the experiences that sculpt us and the knocks that batter us, and the influences exerted on us by all manner of other people with their own conditioning and their own bruises, we generally lose sight of our *true colours*; in other words we lose touch with our true psycho-spiritual identity, or our most essential self. This is because this essence, these true colours (which, as you will discover, is more than a figure of speech) are buried somewhere deep down, in the unconscious part of ourselves where most of our latent power is contained. Our "stuff" – our unresolved difficulties and pains – gets in the way of real communication with ourselves. When we begin to clear these issues and find these *colours* again, we can re-discover the unlimited power of our true potential and begin to realise all sorts of forgotten dreams.

This is an exciting time to be alive, but it is also a challenging and demanding time. The Berlin Wall has come down, bringing together East and West – the greatest division, through opposing belief systems, in our time – by peaceful acceptance, in a way and on a scale that has probably never before been achieved in the history of this planet. So have many of the less tangible walls that divided us: those erected by our institutions and our belief systems, for example; and not just as societies but as individuals. While these walls, these firm structures, kept us apart, they also sometimes gave us the illusion of stability. There is not much left in the way of certainty in the outside world: we have to look inside ourselves for it. Many of the big decisions now are over to us. The sharp points and clear-cut lines of logic and abstraction have dimmed. The left and right hemispheres of the brain are meeting and working together as we all discover – women and men – that we can be round not square; pastel as well as primary. Men, if they wish to, can be nurses or househusbands; they can be seen to care, and wear Pink shirts. Women can be financiers, and run corporations or countries – and even fight for them. Children can be seen **and** heard. Mars and Venus move ever closer, as hi-tech shrinks not just the planet but the cosmos. It's even OK to talk about our feelings! Or is it? Perhaps it's not quite so simple. Just as technology has brought about an exponential rate of outer change, so there are life-changing forces at work within our inner worlds. Perhaps the changing of old traditions and ways of thought is shaking the foundations beneath our feet. Maybe we are not even quite sure, always, of what our feelings really are?

Colours have been woven into the stuff of our lives throughout evolution, with the knowledge of their direct connections to our behaviour known in myriad ways to many civilisations. Colour was used in the healing temples of ancient Egypt, and in ancient India; the first Greek philosopher Pythagoras used it for healing five hundred years before the birth of Christ. Spiritual belief systems of the more recent past, and the rationalism that became dominant over the last few centuries, have played a part in ensuring that colour, as a practical tool for any type of therapy, remained relatively untapped for some time until it began to re-emerge during the course of the twentieth century. In fact, it is remarkable that, while the effects of gamma rays, X-rays, microwaves and other (potentially dangerous) parts of the full spectrum of light have for some time been thoroughly researched and used, the effects of the safe part of that spectrum – the colours that can be perceived by the naked eye – were largely ignored. This is changing. Have no doubt about the power of colour, and the variety of its beneficial effects. Colour and light are finding their way into medical cures; colour signals are used by our own bodies to send information from one cell to another; light and colour are even recognised as the carriers of information from outer space! Colours reflect not just your feelings, but also your thoughts, your memories; and even your state of health. They show you what is significant in your life at the moment; how you are making the important decisions, and how you are responding to what is happening from day to day. They offer you a Pandora's box full of insights that can turn your life around. You will find that your conscious selection of colour can enable you to discover an extraordinary amount about what makes you, and those closest to you, tick. You will find that different colours, which in effect are different wavelengths of light, have a more direct connection with – and powerful influence upon – your thoughts and your feelings than most people have realised. You will discover that the colours you select can guide you towards a better understanding of yourself and your friends than you might ever have imagined in your wildest dreams, because colour and light are an intimate part of your very being! Whatever your race, colour or creed, your truly favourite colours, chosen at any particular moment in your life, uncover the real you, your gifts and strengths, fears and hopes, and hand you a tool for choosing the life you want and living it to the full. Your personal choice of colour clarifies your individual needs, and also your gifts: in doing this, it gives you the power to act consciously instead of just reacting to circumstances; and thus it hands you back the reins to take charge of your own life.

You will learn, through these pages, the beginnings of a skill that will allow you to "read" your personal colour choices, so that you can get a handle on many aspects of yourself and your relationships. You will also discover many practical ways of using colours therapeutically, and simple guidelines for bringing harmony into the living spaces you share, and other colour tools that restore and enhance the companionship between you. You can use colour to keep the home fires burning in your love life; to re-ignite passion where it has faded; to re-fuel the growth of your friendship. Later on you may wish to expand this knowledge from your most intimate relationship and apply it in other areas: your family and social life, and relationships at work.

An understanding of the language of colour, once gained, may be brought as a supporting tool into every context in which you inter-relate with other people. The rewards are limitless. To share your colours with those around you is to bring a new level of joy into your life, where you can rediscover the warmth of real, no-holds-barred, truthful communication; of understanding and being understood. As every child knows, when you feel yourself to be understood you rest in no doubt that you are loved. Understanding and love are the backbone of human growth. It is the support of this backbone that allows you to reach higher and higher: to develop your gifts and ultimately to find the fulfilment of your greatest potential.

Colour? How can something as basic, even prosaic, as colour do all this? If you want to discover how this amazing tool can help you, and enjoy the journey, read on…

PART ONE

WHAT'S THE PROBLEM?

*You cannot teach a man anything; you can only
help him to find it within himself.*

GALILEO

chapter 1

DID I REALLY CHOOSE YOU?

There is a Spanish proverb, which says very justly,
tell me whom you live with, and I will tell you who you are.
Earl of Chesterfield 1694 – 1773

Throughout my late teens and early twenties I watched, with increasing bewilderment, the marriage between my parents. The love between them was a given; it was beyond question. Yet there appeared to be very little of what I recognised as real communication between them; and between them and their children there was next to none.

My father had suffered polio just before he reached the age of twenty, which had left him partially crippled. His limping gait could be heard from some way off. When we heard the sound of the heavy thud approaching from the far end of a corridor we, his children, either froze or looked for a place to hide. It was only much later that I came to understand the reason why he inspired such terror: that some place inside him too, many years before, had frozen; and that he too was looking for somewhere to hide. He existed in his own private world – a kind of prison – of physical discomfort, and emotional pain more ancient than this, which was unresolved and never directly expressed. During the forty years of his marriage, the only person who could reach him was my mother who, through an abundance of the feminine virtues of subtlety, gentleness and generosity, catered unconditionally for his wants and needs. In doing this, she was in line with many others of her generation: she sacrificed absolutely her own talents and desires. These two people were deeply bonded, yet they nevertheless epitomised a world of separation in which the male reigned supreme. It was only some years later, after I watched my mother blossom and flourish in the nine full rich years of her widowhood, that I began to perceive and understand the legacy of love which my father left us; a love which had longed to express itself during his lifetime but which he had scarcely been able to communicate to anyone but her. Little by little, I found compassion, and then gratitude; it was only much later that I came to see not only that I had come to understand something of this generous and very loving man, but also that I resembled him in ways that were not confined only to his more loving, and loveable, aspect....

Meanwhile I had watched, as I say, with bewilderment, and not a little judgment. I knew, or thought I knew, for certain that I would never sacrifice myself in the way that my mother had done. I felt for a time a great anger that the children, like the mother, had been offered up on the altar of this strange union. Then, in the latter half of my twenties – whoops! – I married a man who embodied all those aspects of my father that had caused me the greatest difficulty and pain. It was a few years before I realised what I had done. By this time I had two babies, and was also thoroughly sick. In fact I was in a prison of my own making, which I had chosen – according to the ancient wisdom that has become a contemporary cliché – in order to learn the lessons that some higher, super-conscious part of my nature knew I must learn. We co-habited for seventeen years, sharing houses and children, and experiencing thoughts and feelings which had about as much in common as mercury and granite.

MYSTERY TOUR

My situation was far from unusual. The marriage of Prince Charles and Princess Diana has been described as a disastrous mis-match between two of the most dysfunctional families in the kingdom. Our paths were similar in only this one respect; and, like the Royal Princes and so many others that year, I finally brought my marriage to an end in 1992, escaping with the three children whose lives I hoped to salvage, albeit in dire poverty and with a most uncertain future ahead of us. I embarked then on a journey which would continue for many years, in a determined attempt to discover what it is, for one thing, that draws us into relationship; and how a happy partnership can be not only created, but sustained. I read everything I could lay my hands on; I thought, I talked – for some time rather more than I listened. I trained as a counsellor and later as a teacher in colour therapy and took that as a healing tool to many countries and many people. And then I did listen. I listened and watched with astonishment and fascination as the life stories, the fears and aspirations, the frustrations and hopes of people all over the planet spread themselves before my eyes and my heart in glorious technicolour. Yet ultimately, the search only revealed the full truth of itself as I discovered, little by little, that the direction of this journey was towards my own centre. It led towards what was at first the uncomfortable recognition that the single constant in all our relationships is what we bring to it, which is ourselves.

I discovered that we come into relationship to find not an *outer* but an *inner* solution to the problems of our existence; that intimate relationship, in particular, was never intended as a passport to instant happiness, but is instead – and much more excitingly – a mystery tour. What a wonderful gift the British Royal family had offered to the world: it became clear that a dysfunctional family could offer us a better education, if we were open to it, than we were likely to find for miles around! The misfortunes of a family in public life have perhaps offered an opportunity to people the world over to part the net curtains on their own domestic scene: to realise that family life is as often a battleground as a haven of peace, and that there are good reasons for this. Our family lives challenge us to face the totality of ourselves: not just the angels within us, but the demons as well.

For a time, for all its outer activity, my journey was a lonely one. It was only when I had accepted and even embraced the solitude of the path I had chosen, and my unequivocal need to take responsibility for whatever I had created, that I found that this very same road led me to a relationship which is as joyful and creative as my previous one was desolate and destructive. Although the social landscape changes from one generation to the next, beneath the view that we see from the surface, the laws that govern the universe remain the same. This does not mean that human beings are unable to evolve: it means the very opposite. The rules of the game remain unchanged; but as we learn those rules and improve our skills, we get better at playing the game.

The freedom and the exhilaration of living at this moment in history comes partly from the tools that are being unearthed which offer us the opportunity to understand some of these natural laws, or principles; and, through this understanding, to undo the cycles of human experience which in the past have limited and bound us. There is certainly a crisis facing many people in close personal relationships worldwide. But the very word "crisis", as it occurs in Eastern languages, contains two characters: one of these means danger, and the other, a hidden opportunity. This hidden opportunity is the gift that offers us the possibility of fulfilment within our close partnerships and friendships which I know I should envy if I were standing in the shoes of my grandmother and looking upon life in the twenty-first century. It is exactly the difficulties between us that provide the material for us to find a new and deeper level of interaction.

We are being challenged to talk to each other; to break down the barriers between us and find a new quality of communication which has the potential to extend to human relationships everywhere. The possibility at this time in history, as more and more understanding is discovered and information spreads at the speed of light, is for us to make quantum leaps in our awareness and in our ability to connect with one another. In discovering some of the forces that make us tick, we are enabled to exert choices and to find, in the words of an anonymous

It is exactly the difficulties between us that provide the material for us to find a new and deeper level of interaction

prayer, *"the courage to change those things we can change; the serenity to accept those things we cannot change; and the wisdom to know the difference".*

To work therapeutically with colour is to find, at the very least, a signpost towards this courage, this serenity and this wisdom. I have worked for some years both as a counsellor and as a teacher, using predominantly one method of colour therapy, which is known as Aura-Soma. This work has taken me to many different parts of the globe, and brought me into deeply personal contact with people of many languages and cultures. If ever I had needed confirmation, this was proof indeed that the messages contained within colour and light are universal, cutting right through the education, conditioning, personality and other layers with which we consciously and unconsciously surround ourselves, to arrive at the heart of the matter.

The method derived by that particular colour school, Aura-Soma, revolves around the client's personal choice of colour: a client is invited to choose a small selection of those colours which attract him, or her, the most. This is of central importance. It is in consciously choosing the colours with which you resonate that you find yourself gazing into a mirror which reflects the reality of who you are; and as you begin to recognise more deeply that reality, you can take back the reins to direct the course of your own life.

It was while I was working with students and clients as individuals that the potential for extending the benefits of colour insights to couples, and indeed to our relationships within families and in the wider context of work, powerfully presented itself. There followed an exciting exploration, and I am grateful to those couples who have felt able to come and share their experience. The stories that will follow throughout the text are, for the main part, composites; gathered up from these multi-cultural threads that have made up the broad, and rather odd, tapestry of my experience throughout the 1990s. (The English names they all bear within the text are merely a convention.)

When people undergo colour counselling as a couple, therefore, the core of the consultation is the colour selections which they make individually, and which are then looked at in combination; in other words, the colour choices each person has made are examined simultaneously with, and in relation to, the choices of their partner or friend. For the purposes of this book, which will show in the simplest and most practical way possible how you may bring an understanding of colour into the dynamics of your personal interactions, an array of single colours is sufficient (information is briefly offered in Chapter 12 on the more comprehensive, and more complex, selection of Aura-Soma dual-colour bottles which I use for teaching and counselling). In the colour plates near the centre of the book (Fig. 4, pp. 100–1), you will find a range of some of the best-recognised colours in the rainbow spectrum. At the front and back of this book, you will find these colours repeated in the form of cards which you can cut out and use to make a pack or a spectrum of colours, when you come to look at the significance of your own colour preferences. Soon you can begin to look at these preferences – your own and those of other people – and discover what they mean. We will go on, later, to explore the ways in which colour can act as a guide, or perhaps even a torch, which highlights the source of some of these difficulties.

First, however, let us look briefly at some of the background against which people everywhere are struggling to come to terms with the multiple challenges in their communications with the people they love the most. This is best achieved by looking at an example: here is one couple's story, which illustrates themes common to many of us.

Sam and Anita

Once both parties to the consultation are confident that they have made a firm selection of the colours that most attract them, one of the first questions I often ask of them is how they came to meet. This is a simple but useful starting point which serves, among other purposes, to remind people about their basic connection. Sam and Anita had met some seven or eight years previously in Hong Kong, where he was working in a corporate bank and she was taking a year out, after finishing her degree course, travelling around Asia. When they were introduced by mutual friends, they discovered that Anita's cousin had been quite a close friend of Sam's in the southern English town where they had also both spent a portion of their young lives.

Sam and Anita had been experiencing major conflict. Here – in a look at the circumstances of their coming to know one another – was something apparently quite trivial, but which reminded them of their immediate source of similar experiences, and of the warm sense of security in which their friendship had originally grown. This then prepares the ground for two important questions, which will most likely come later, during the process of exploring the messages within the colours they have chosen.

1 *What characteristics have played the largest part in attracting them to that other person?*
2 *What have been the major hurdles for them in their most intimate relationships in the past or present?*

In the majority of cases, sexual attraction plays a central part in the initial attraction. This is a given. What is useful is to begin to find out what it is, apart from the obvious, more superficial factors, that underlies the attraction to one person rather than to another. And here, there is a clear pattern that emerges, much more often than not. It is those same qualities that attract us towards another person which also provide some of the major difficulties as the relationship develops.

As the difficulties surface, there begins an insidious erosion of the ground on which the relationship is built. Anita, for example, said that the characteristics that had attracted her the most towards Sam were his strength, his projective, protective quality of masculine energy and his capacity for dynamic and clear thinking. Sam said that he had been drawn to Anita's spontaneity, to her innovative and creative gifts, to her warmth and her generosity. When they were asked to identify the major areas of difficulty with one another, Anita said that Sam was very controlling, too busy to listen to her properly and that he frequently missed the subtleties and the enjoyment of the moment that she wanted to share with him; that he was so busy doing and controlling that he missed out on real living. Sam said that he had found Anita to be selfish and unreliable, never making plans and frequently disappearing at no notice after some project or person that had caught her immediate attention. He said that she gave too much of herself indiscriminately to whoever wanted her time; so that he had come to feel that she put little value on him and was never available for him anyway.

Each of these two people had clearly been attracted towards the other by qualities which contrasted with their own. Anita and Sam had both been drawn towards something in the other that they *lacked* in themselves. Unconsciously, each had been looking to the other to complete what they perceived as insufficient (or lacking) within themselves; and each had also – and equally

> *It is those same qualities that attract us towards another person which also provide some of the major difficulties as the relationship develops.*

unconsciously – seized the opportunity offered by the other to *extend their own limits* and grow nearer to their potential. But, as time went on and the relationship grew and changed, it was at least some of these very characteristics in their partner that had proved extremely difficult for either of them to cope with in the daily context of living together. Sam's "strength" and his "protective, projective, masculine" quality was one side of a coin whose flip side was a tendency to want to be in control. Anita thoroughly appreciated Sam's successes at work, and the freedom this left her to explore her own interests without having to concern herself too much about her timetable or her earning power; but when, as he generally did, Sam insisted on keeping sole charge of the TV controller as well as the bank account, and on driving her car as well as his own, rather than allow her to sit behind the wheel, she wanted to scream. Sam, for his part, saw and even sometimes envied Anita's creative and artistic talent; but he was frustrated by the stream of ideas that he felt were never going anywhere concrete. He also liked the warmth and easy grace which seemed to draw people towards Anita and make close friendship rather easier for her than it had generally been for him; but he became very resentful when this same ease and open-hearted quality in her nature threatened to remove her from him.

So much for the differences between them. Sam and Anita had been drawn together from the start, not only by these differences but, as we have seen, by the common ground of their respective histories. This was deeper than just the town of their childhood and a tenuous family connection. Some similarities in their background had given rise to several traits in which they resembled one another. These two individuals both came from well-to-do business families, where the parents had been proud of the achievements they had made by their own efforts and enterprise. The children in both families had been encouraged to believe that, through a mixture of alacrity and diligence, they could create whatever they chose. Anita and Sam, in consequence, were both quite marked individualists who had been accustomed to putting their own signature on whatever they were involved in. Sam was the only child of parents who had perhaps been over-protective, but who had in any case pandered to all his wants and needs, and who also expected great things of him. There had always been some pressure on him to excel. Anita was the youngest child of four, and the only girl; in a more rowdy context, she too had been given a special place. She had been a quick and able child, and she readily described herself as a spoilt brat. They had both, each in their different ways, been encouraged towards achievement. While Sam leaned towards the material and the practical, and Anita aspired more towards people, painting, ideas and travel, they both had a tendency to involve themselves completely in whatever occupied them in the present moment; and they were both capable of some considerable impatience. They had each recognised and enjoyed the other's sense of power until this very quality in them caused them to lock horns. At this point, other qualities in both of them, such as their intolerance and their expectation of having their own will satisfied, rose to the surface.

At present, both Sam and Anita had completely lost touch with anything that had brought them together. They were finding it near-impossible to communicate in any way. "Poles apart", it was as though each of them had become locked within their own universe, unable to perceive or understand anything of the world which their partner inhabited. For months, even years, the ocean that divided them had been growing wider and wider. Anita, increasingly frustrated by Sam's conservative nature and his apparent coldness, had found her natural impulsiveness and impatience getting the better of her. Her bouts of rage, which had at first evoked some kind of response in Sam, now drove him more deeply into his own corner. Sam's quiet sobriety, which had previously been so solid and reassuring to Anita, now presented itself to her in a different way: she saw him as boring and rigid. While he withdrew into a safe but sterile and solitary life of hard work, punctuated by meals and highlighted only by successful deals on the stock exchange, Anita began wandering further afield, staying away for longer periods of time. Sam was unsure about where she stayed, or even whom she might be staying with, and Anita's refusal to give him an answer to this was pushing him to the limits of his frustration (and anxiety), as he felt her slipping from his grasp. Instead, she talked about her business plans: projects that vaguely combined her fine arts training with her desire to run a small company. Though Anita had poured energy into these ideas, she had kept changing course and none of her projects had yet materialised into anything tangible or productive.

Intimate relationship can be the most healing, or "wholeing" experience of a person's life. It teaches you a whole lot about where you are coming from. But all healing involves the lancing of old wounds. It involves the shedding of all sorts of emotional toxins that have previously, even if unconsciously, hindered your development and your achievements. In other words it brings to the surface buried pain and unresolved issues that you may previously have attempted to ignore or forget. The deeper the intimacy the more "stuff" is likely to come up, and this tends to manifest as something very unlike the love which brought it into the daylight.

Intimate relationship, far from being the safe haven you may hope for, is more likely to challenge you at the most profound level, and bring you face to face with many of your earliest wounds, many of which have hitherto lain in the deep recesses of your unconscious.

When you can let go of the fear and trust yourself and one another, new horizons open up in front of you: it is the very intimacy of close relationships which can provide you with the central and most significant opportunity for self-

> *Intimate relationship, far from being the safe haven you may hope for, is more likely to challenge you at the most profound level, and bring you face to face with many of your earliest wounds, many of which have hitherto lain in the deep recesses of your unconscious.*

This clarity enables you to find a new and much deeper equilibrium.

discovery and knowledge. It is through your interactions with others, and in particular through your closest friendships and personal bonds, that you can be brought to the clearest recognition of who you are, what you are, why you are; and even – and here is the greatest gift that any of us can give and receive in close relationship – what it is that you have the possibility of *becoming*, so that you can begin to fulfil the potential that so often lies unused. The very lancing of old wounds, and the consequent release of what might be described as emotional pus, that happens in close relationship is exactly what enables those wounds to heal, so that you can grow much more fully into whatever it is that you have the potential to be. When you look in a mirror and see a simple and clear reflection of the way things are, you can let go of illusion, self-deception and judgment: together, and to whatever varying degree, these have kept you (or me, or anyone else) stuck at one end or another of a pole, from where, previously, you may have separated yourself further by approaching others in the same spirit of judgment that you have offered yourself. This clarity enables you to find a new and much deeper equilibrium.

Your relationships can then become the ground for the deepest nurturing and growth. Colour, once you contemplate it, provides that mirror; and so, however unwittingly, do your partners and friends. Colour is the expression of light; and the energies of light, like the warm rays of sunshine in summer, work gently, dissolving fear so that you find the compassion, for yourself and others, that begins at home. Through the people closest to you, you have the opportunity to discover and face not only the pain of your difficulties and weaknesses, but also – which is the great reward – the strengths and talents which often remain undiscovered while you are alone.

At any stage in the history of a relationship with any person who is close to you, where there is willingness and a degree of commitment, light and colour can be brought to your aid, gently dissolving the blocks to your communication with yourself and each other, so that the energy which is necessary for communication courses around you, and through you, and between you once more. Restored and invigorated, both parties can move towards each other, and come to a balance between your differences. The differences then become a source of stimulation and fun: instead of finding yourselves set in the kind of stone that may sometimes have paralysed your communications in the past, you can move and stretch out again. Eventually you can discover the much deeper unity that underlies the differences between you, but this only becomes possible once you have acknowledged and worked with whatever it is that makes you individuals. Then you can discover the real joy that comes when a relationship is a living, moving flow of energy between people who are enjoying the dance.

Sam and Anita, at this time, however, still had some way to go. They could have been well described as ice and steam. Part Three will take up their story from time to time through their selections of colour. The important point here is to understand the nature of the polarities that divided them.

What was going on? Sam and Anita, like most of the rest of us at one time or another, were in the grip of quite powerful forces which they did not understand. Let's forget about individual stories for the moment, and go a bit further back to somewhere near the beginning...

chapter 2

A WORLD OF OPPOSITES

(Love and fear) are the opposite ends of the great polarity
which I created when I produced the universe

Neale Donald Walsch

Conversations with God

I t is interesting to reflect that, as the moment of birth approaches, it is the baby, and not the mother who has housed the baby, who releases the hormone that triggers this process. This means that, like every other human being, at some level you chose to get on with it and be born. This passage away from the warm safety of the womb catapulted you, some years ago no doubt, from the reassuring monotony of warmth and sensation which had characterised your conscious experience up until then, and – ouch! – into a world of opposites.

These opposites are an inevitable part of physical life: light and dark, hot and cold, hunger and satisfaction, sound and silence. As time went on, the opposites became more complex: peace and conflict, joy and sorrow, passion and discipline, male and female; and many others. You found yourself faced with the tricky task, as you began to mature, of attempting to keep these opposites in a healthy state of balance. The fact that you appear to have chosen this journey may remind you that this world of opposites, or polarities, not only surrounded and still surrounds you, to comprise your outer experience, but it is also contained within you, as your very nature. We could say that you released that birth hormone because you wanted to grow and learn and discover; you wanted to explore and be free. But human beings, unanimously, are ambivalent by nature: you also wanted safety and security.

This experience of polarised forces – both around us and within us – constitutes one of the cardinal laws, or principles, on which our universe is based. Perhaps, in the context of our relationships, one of the vital aspects of this duality is our nature both as separate and sacred individuals on the one hand, and as social beings on the other. Our solitariness and our social nature are equally essential and inevitable parts of the package. This brings us to two vital truths:

1 *We cannot have true communion with others unless we also know ourselves as separate individuals. And conversely:*

2 *The most powerful route towards this essential self-knowledge is to be found in the close relationships that we share with the people with whom we share our lives.*

It is a well-known business maxim that the essential pre-requisite for successful negotiation is an understanding of where the other person is coming from. This principle is equally fundamental to any healthy personal relationship. We could extend such a maxim, to say that the golden rule for successful negotiation with *yourself* is to understand where *you* are coming from: in other words, it is not enough to try to alter your behaviour; you have to understand the cause of that behaviour before you are in a position to modify it. When you find such an understanding, first for yourself and later for one another (it can only happen this way round), through the mirror of colour, you are quite likely to discover that underneath your differences there lies the possibility of a deeper unity than you had suspected.

Balance

Colour, when used as a diagnostic tool, has the capacity to illustrate what those polarities are that seem to divide you; and at the same time to demonstrate both your complementarity and your shared origins and concerns. Certain colours, like certain people, may be described as "opposites"; and these same colours are also complementary: they contain the potential not only to resolve these opposing characteristics, but also to support and complement one another. Before any of the contradictions in your life are resolved, however, directly contrasting realities surround you and suffuse you. And every time the scales are tipped to one end or the other – you become a workaholic, say, and forget how to take time out – you get out of balance; both within yourself and between one another.

Your conscious choices of colour can show you the aspects in which you are particularly out of kilter, both individually and in relation to each other; and then they can show you the possibilities for redressing the balance. More often than not, you will discover that the process of searching for this mutual understanding takes the friendship or partnership to a deeper equilibrium than you would ever have found had the problem not arisen in the first place.

At the time that Sam and Anita, who were mentioned in the previous chapter, came to me for advice and support, it was very clear that they were both some way off their own internal balance, as well as a long distance away from any kind of harmony in the way they related to one another. Anita, it has been suggested, could have been described as all passion and steam, while Sam, at present, had resorted to a strict self-imposed discipline and, in fact, he felt as lonely as ice. Neither extreme was sufficient on its own to create an integrated life. Passion without discipline evaporates like steam; without form or shape, its heat can destroy what is around it while also dissipating itself. Discipline without passion, on the other hand, is like painting by numbers: the structure is there, but it lacks the creative force that gives it life. It is not surprising that, on the one hand, Anita had recently suffered two or three fevers, and that, on the other, Sam was attempting to fend off a depression which was severe enough to impact quite severely on his work. There was plenty of material to draw on, however, in the re-forging of this relationship.

Centrifugal v. centripetal forces

Our journey from conception into independence offers us all sorts of exciting possibilities, but it also fills us with trepidation. From our very beginning, we are subject to two opposing forces: the expansive push towards greater autonomy, freedom and independence; and the contractual pulling back towards the security of what we already know. We are like plants that push our stalks further and further towards the light, and simultaneously deepen our roots into the nurturing darkness of the earth below us. Or, we could borrow a term from physics to describe these two forces: the outward movement can be seen as the centrifugal force, the inward movement as the centripetal one, both of them acting on all levels of our inclinations and our behaviour.

These opposing forces, of course, play a significant part in our relationships, and in what draws us into those relationships. On the one hand we are attracted to the *opposite* of whatever we are. We know instinctively that, as individuals, we are incomplete; and the thrust onward and outward is, in part, the drive towards the greater and greater fulfilment of our potential, as we push the boundaries, constantly testing ourselves to expand our own limits. Simultaneously, we are reassured by what is *familiar*: that which is already known protects us from the arduousness of constant effort; it affords us the security of what has already been experienced and understood.

Both of these tendencies are fundamental to the nature of every one of us, and both have a down side! They are likely to come into play at different times in your life, shaking you awake, usually by making you uncomfortable, if not downright mad. The "centrifugal" force, the drive to expand and venture into unknown territory, soon brings you up against some of your most fundamental fears: one of these is the fear of separation; another is the fear of inequality. If someone is different from you, then, for one thing, you may feel yourself to be in danger of loneliness; and, for another, they might have something you have not got. They might be richer or more beautiful. They might be cleverer or luckier. History is the story of conflict between those with differences: white versus black, woman against man, Catholic versus Protestant, shortage versus plenty, and so on. In a close relationship, those very aspects you had perhaps espoused because they complemented you, making you feel stronger and more complete, can turn swiftly into something that appears to threaten you. This is the moment at which love so often begins to turn to fear: the giving and caring declines into a mutual struggle for power, as the story of Anita and Sam started to illustrate.

This is one scenario: the attraction of opposites. There is also another scenario that occurs, usually simultaneously. This arises out of the opposing, or "centripetal", force: your attraction to whatever is familiar in other people. You may be drawn to whatever is familiar, because it makes you feel comfortable and safe. Sam and Anita were drawn together partly by the similarity of some of their roots; and their own similarities, as you have seen, went further than this, into resemblances in their upbringing and in some of their characteristics and expectations. What happens in this situation is that, even though you often do not realise it, the other person is *mirroring* to you something of yourself. People are drawn towards mirrors because there is a natural human tendency to look at oneself. This is all well and good while you see in your friend or loved one a reflection of what you like and accept in yourself. Later, however, the mirror starts to show you some other things, and you will begin to come up against the parts of yourself you had chosen to ignore or deny because you did not like those parts.... Mirrors have a lot to do with light; and where there is light, there is also the shadow. Every colour in the rainbow comes from light; and the messages within colour also contain a "shadow" aspect: in other words a darker and more difficult side. In looking at the "mirror" that a close friend or loved one holds up for you, part of what you will eventually see is your own shadow; or that aspect of your own *true colours* that you have wanted to suppress or reject. Here again, love may be in danger of turning to something rather different: resentment, perhaps, or worse.

But there is a great gift in facing the fullness of yourself, with all your shadows and fears: the journey towards self-knowledge is also the journey to a greater freedom than you have ever known. This freedom repercusses on your relationships. So not only do you come to know yourself through your close interaction with others, but also – and here is the good news: the more deeply you know yourself, the better are your chances of fulfilment and success within your close interactions.

> *The more deeply you know yourself, the better are your chances of fulfilment and success within your close interactions.*

Close relationship offers you the opportunity for the real communication that comes when you let go of the fear that has divided you in the past, when you may have found yourself set in concrete within an identity or a mindset that perhaps a part of you did not even want. These opposing forces bring you face to face – and this is crucial – with the polarities, or states of imbalance, within *yourself.* For, before people get out of touch with one another, they have already become out of touch with many parts of themselves! The further you tip the scales to one end or the other within your own psyche, and therefore move out of your own equilibrium – on all levels: your heart, your soul, your body, your mind – the more surely do you attract towards you other people who are similarly lop-sided! You, and they, are drawn to that mirror again – each other – and quite often with disastrous results.

Disharmony is simply the moving of forces out of a state of equilibrium and into imbalance. And imbalance, or disharmony, generally causes problems. This apparently simple, natural law of

Disharmony is simply the moving of forces out of a state of equilibrium and into imbalance.

polarity, or opposites, pervades all our experience. When things slip out of balance, like a see-saw that has become weighted down at one end, you are – though you may not have realised it – unable to move. This is when you can very easily feel overwhelmed, helpless and resentful. **Wherever a relationship is not working, the movement of energy between two people becomes blocked.** There is no motion, no flow, and the dynamics between you begin to turn to stone. Both parties to a relationship become stuck, unable to reach out and touch each other, as communication grinds to a halt. This may happen quite suddenly, as a result of a major clash. More often, it happens quietly and insidiously: you awaken to the dawning realisation that, somehow or other, you have slipped out of reach of each other; that the concrete became set while you were otherwise engaged. With no flow of energy moving between you, there is none moving around you either, and this fossilisation inevitably spreads into every aspect of your life: your work, your bank balance, your sex life, your health.

Obviously, people differ in their tendency to expand or to stay with what they know. Some of us have married – so to speak – the boy next door, while others have explored the very heart of foreign continents and people. In all relationships, there is a mixture of the familiar and the unknown. But there is a common factor that applies universally to our partnerships and friendships: when we enter any kind of close union, we are generally unprepared for the flip side of those things that first attracted us – either by their difference from us or by the safety they offered. A relationship that has any depth at all will soon bring our own *true colours*, or our real nature, to the surface. Self-evident as this may seem, it is crucial, and often overlooked when we are busy blaming "him", "her" or "them" for every frustrating circumstance we encounter. Yet, it is exactly these tests, as time progresses, that challenge both members in a pair, or indeed people in any situation in which we are living or working together, to expand our awareness and our understanding. It is exactly these tests that challenge us to talk to each other! They provide an opportunity for us to get to know both ourselves and one another on a very much deeper level than we could ever have done if our true colours had been able (which they cannot do in close relationship) to remain hidden away.

The communication that these tests challenge us to find is essential if we are to approach a state of equilibrium, which ultimately is the goal of all healing, in every context. It is essential if we are to avoid the downward slide into the kind of conflict that can rapidly become destructive. Communication is the only means by which we can establish a ground of trust within which a partnership can grow and thrive. Communication sometimes requires hard work. It is made much easier when we see one another through the light of colour.

Colour also helps us to reach beyond the polar opposites which have so often kept us divided. The problem with our perception of opposites is that we put labels on what we experience. These labels often imply some kind of judgment (good or bad, beautiful or ugly, right or wrong and so on). When we are in a position of judgment, we remain separated from whatever it is that we are judging, and thus alone: hence, for one example, the age-old separation between man and woman. **The reason why colour helps us to overcome the divisions between us is that colour comes from light**, and light takes us, according not only to mystics but also even to contemporary scientific theory, right back to our own beginning: to the source of our very nature. This is why, where conventional psychotherapy addresses the psyche, or the mind, colour and light – coming from the sun, or "sol" – appears, from empirical evidence through the ages, to communicate with the deeper aspect of ourselves, or the "soul". Thanks to the efforts of twentieth-century scientists, we can now begin to see how this comes about.

From Light to Matter

The energy of light forms the building blocks of physical life as we know it. At a fundamental level, the physical world evolves from light energy, which lowers its vibration sufficiently to condense into what we recognise as matter. This is an over-simplified description of our highly complex and ever-expanding universe, in which galaxies are moving further and further apart, and the objects in our solar system revolve around the swirling mass of exploding helium that we call the sun; and where the ultimate extreme of matter is a black hole, in which state mass cannot get enough of itself. Nevertheless, the bottom line is that this is true, and this truth has practical consequences which affect us much more than we have been aware. The physicist Dr David Bohm, reminding us that we and all other material forms are made up of light, has written that: *"light is energy and it is also information – content, form and structure. It is the potential for everything."* Deepak Chopra describes the *"nonstuff that make(s) up everything that we consider stuff or matter"* of the universe as *"impulses of energy and information"*. In fact, *"the stuff of the universe"*, Chopra says, *"is nonstuff"*. (*Creating Affluence*, Deepak Chopra, Bantam Press.) It is of great help to us if we grasp the truth of this statement when working with colour.

COLOUR AND INTUITION

Your head (or your intellect) is very necessary, but in any attempt to understand yourself or another person, your heart, or some part of you that functions beyond the limited confines of the rational mind, plays an even more vital part. The energies of colour can take you *beyond the intellect*, which is the faculty in you that labels and categorises (and which therefore understands the world in terms of opposites: tall or short, near or far, cruel or kind and so on). They take you into the realm of your other vital faculty, which lies beyond and beneath this world of labels, division and judgment. This faculty is the *intuition*, the inner teaching which comes from that aspect of you which knows *directly*, which experiences directly, and which can therefore show you a way back to unity. The intuition is recognised within Zen Buddhist philosophy as man's highest faculty of perception. The in-tuition is the teaching which, first, comes from the innermost aspect of yourself and which then enables you to understand a concept or an experience *from the inside*.

While the intellect relates predominantly to knowledge that you have learned from teachers and books and so on, the intuition is allied more closely to wisdom, or experiential knowledge. A mother *knows* how her small child feels, long before that child is able to communicate through words with the outside world. A nurse knows when her patient is entering the terminal phase of an illness. A child knows when its parents are unhappy together, no matter how cleverly those parents work to create a happy atmosphere. When you approach another person through the light of colour, you do indeed engage the intellect, or the mind, but the more familiar you become with the messages of colour, the more easily can you also move beyond and beneath the intellect, and into the realms where intuition rules; which means that you know and experience directly – just like the mother with her young child, or the husband who is well tuned into the thoughts and feelings of his wife. This means that, through colour, you have the opportunity of knowing and experiencing directly at least something of what another person is living.

This means that, through colour, you have the opportunity of knowing and experiencing directly at least something of what another person is living.

You do not have to be a person's mother or husband to know something of that other person directly if he shows you his truly favourite colours. If you come to me and ask me to interpret your selection of colours, my intellect will quickly present me with a number of possibilities that are familiar to me from my knowledge of what various colours mean. An initial glance at your selection shows me your first choice. Suppose, just as an example, that this first colour chosen is Gold. This is only the beginning of the picture, but your choice of this hue may at once suggest to my mind (or intellect, or head) that your disposition is sunny – not sad; that your intelligence is swift – not sluggish; that you are discerning – not naïve. This is because I have learned the associations made between these concepts and the colour Gold.

When we bring colour into the realm of attempting to understand ourselves and one another, however, we work from compassion rather than from the textbook. So when I look at your colour preferences, my intuition will see beyond this dualistic construction of the intellect, which has taught me these "Gold" possibilities. It is the intuition that exists within the world of colour and light, and which enables me to experience directly at least something of what you are. Beyond the words that my intellectual faculty can use to describe your state of mind and heart, your positive and negative attributes, **my intuition can simply allow me to be in your energy space**, so that I know – directly – at least something of the reality that you experience. It is the intuition

When we bring colour into the realm of attempting to understand ourselves and one another, however, we work from compassion rather than from the textbook.

that causes me to *feel* your joy, your confusion and fears, your wisdom, your weakness and your power. While I shall convey to you these perceptions in words, the perceptions themselves are more akin to those of poetry and painting than to prose. How, then, can I fail to be with you in com-passion? And the same, of course, applies to you, when you begin to look at those close to you through these new and different lenses: i.e. through the colour selections that these people may make. Working with light takes us away from the intellect and into a place of intuition where we know and experience directly, which makes compassion – and therefore empathy – automatic.

Working with light takes us away from the intellect and into a place of intuition where we know and experience directly, which makes compassion – and therefore empathy – automatic.

This is the reason why the energies of light and colour, gentle though they are in the way they work, are so powerful in their ability to reach beyond the conflicts and divisions and show us the profound interconnection that exists between us.

Colour is absolutely fundamental to our life on earth; it is also an integral part of what we are, and its influence on us is profound. When my daughter Magdalen was six, she was hit by a car, and was not expected to live. Thanks to many miracles (not the least of which was the skill of the surgeon and the intensive and loving care of the nurses), she survived. During the months that followed there were many signs that she was in close touch with her higher consciousness, or her soul; and that because of this she was acutely aware of many of her needs, as her body struggled to heal. One of the most surprising things about this phase in her recovery was her determination and her clarity about the colours she needed to wear. When she first arrived home, she was unable to speak, and was only able to walk with assistance; but every morning she crawled around among the many clothes I offered her, showing clear anxiety until she found the only two colours she was prepared to wear (a Violet T-shirt and a Pink pair of leggings). It soon became evident that this one set of clothes must be washed every night, until she was prepared to move on to other colours, which she did about a month later. She was similarly alert to the colours of the foods she wanted, pointing, as we shopped, to items such as Red, Yellow and Green peppers, brightly coloured berries, and Red meats.

This was an extreme situation of a person struggling for life. The opposite extreme can also occur. Look, for example, at Susan, a patient in a psychiatric ward. Here was someone who left her job, abandoned her baby and sank into the deepest clinical depression, numb to all life and light. Her world became, quite literally, grey: she was unable to perceive any colour in her surroundings. She had shut down on all levels and was unable to receive even the first gift of life, which is light. This is not an unusual symptom in those who, for whatever reasons and pressures, have no wish to be here. In such a state, the person finds that grief and sadness have washed all the colour from their life.

These contrasting sketches illustrate the truth which – although it is still only imperfectly understood – is nevertheless now recognised, not only by mystics and healers, but by the scientific establishment: that colour is intimately connected with that very force which is life itself.

Before we go on to look at some of the specific messages that different colours have for us, we need to take a brief look at the field of light-energy in constant motion, which is the universe we inhabit, and which is also ourselves. An understanding of this phenomenon makes it much easier to find an intuitive feeling for the gentle and powerful way in which, through colour, we are enabled to recognise both ourselves and one another; to dissolve the blockages within us and between us; and to create mutual communication which is conscious and dynamic.

chapter 3

ARE WE ON THE SAME WAVELENGTH?

If a man will begin with certainties,
he shall end in doubts;
but if he will be content to begin with doubts,
he shall end in certainties.

Francis Bacon

We know that our thoughts and feelings move and change from one moment to another; but we have generally assumed that our physical bodies are solid and reasonably stable, changing only very gradually as we move from childhood towards old age. In reality, things are not quite as hard and fast, as reassuringly substantial, as we once thought – before Einstein, and quantum physics, turned even our rational thinking upside down. Your body is not static, nor even particularly solid; and neither are its boundaries as clearly defined by the skin as you may have believed. This body, like the rest of the living world, is, rather, light energy which has condensed to a much lower – or slower – level of vibration than the energy around it, but which is nevertheless in constant motion.

The consequence of this movement of light energy is that, on the one hand, you are continuously receiving light waves that move towards you; and on the other it means that you are also radiating light waves into the energy field around and beyond you. The significance of this is that light energy is intimately bound up with the phenomenon of colour. You learned at school that what you perceive as colour is the product of pure light: that each of the different hues shown in the rainbow is a division of White light. Are you aware that different colours appeal to you at different times; that they have different associations in your mind, and that you have clear preferences regarding the colours you choose to wear or put into your home?

These preferences are more significant than you have probably realised. Because the electromagnetic spectrum of light is a gradation of altering wavelengths, each colour, like each note of music, has its own wavelength, or vibrational rate. This denotes its particular character: it might well be described as its signature. Colours have different "vibes". We human (or hue-man) beings also have different "vibes"

There is a level at which you express your unique personal quality, your individuality, as colour. You will both attract and radiate those colours which, for various reasons, resonate most specifically with you. Vicky Wall, the clairvoyant founder of Aura-Soma colour therapy, said often that *"you are the colours you choose; and the colours you choose reflect your being's needs"*. If, at the most funda-

> *Colours have different "vibes".*
> *We human (or hue-man) beings*
> *also have different "vibes".*

mental level, you are derived from light energy, it follows that you have your own particular vibrational rate. When you say that someone has "good vibes", or is "right on your wavelength", what you actually mean is that this person's *true colour*, or predominant vibrational wavelength, harmonises with your own!

This colour, this light-energy, is – remember – in constant motion. You are, therefore, a part of a continuous flow of light, or in other words colour, which moves around and through you and those with whom you interact. This is not simply an abstract idea, but a physical, or more accurately an energetic, reality. A way to imagine this is to compare it with the air in a room full of people, which moves gently around that room as it enters and leaves each person, in a perpetual flow of breath. There is something of a problem, however, in conveying the concept of this coloured field of light: most of us cannot see it….We do, however, sense it in another way. Like so many aspects of our lives that we take for granted, it comes to our attention more forcibly at times when we are in great need.

Richard

Look, for instance, at Richard, a sixteen year old child whose family suddenly lost all their money through the activities of a fraudulent business partner: they had to sell their home, the mother became ill, and Richard was removed from the fee-paying school where he had been absorbed in every aspect of school life, to live in a flat in the nearest town and complete his education. The first thing that he did in this flat was to paint the walls of his room Orange. He had not previously liked this colour at all, and he was surprised to find that he had suddenly surrounded himself in it. Here is an example of a situation that causes a person to crave a particular colour: in this case the colour is Orange, and it has been shown time and again in practice that this ray very frequently comes up in cases of injury or emotional shock. Shock can cause our life force to leak from the lower abdominal area, to which the colour Orange applies (see "The Chakras" and "The Aura" overleaf). Richard needed, quite literally, that particular wavelength of light – the colour Orange – to resonate in his environment, to help him to restore his balance. In general, children are still in close touch with their instinctive, intuitive side: they easily, although unconsciously, select exactly those colours that they need for whatever it is that they are experiencing at that moment.

To understand how the perpetual movement of light waves applies to us in a practical way, we need to borrow the wisdom and understanding from the East which has only in recent years become anything like common knowledge to those of us living in the contemporary, rational and science-based world of the West. We need to refer briefly to phenomena such as the "chakras" and the "aura", those generally unseen aspects of our physiology which exist as an energy field around the physical body. They are more often than not unseen because, at this point in our evolution, there is only a relatively small number of people who are able to perceive vibrations of light that exist outside the spectrum which is visible to the average human eye. There is nothing magic about people who are able to see these wavelengths: it is as simple as the fact that dogs easily hear sounds that are too high-pitched for the human ear to pick up. As all forms of life are changing and evolving all the time, it is not really surprising that increasing numbers of people are able to perceive these energy fields.

Until comparatively recently, we were largely dependent, for the confirmation that this subtle anatomy exists, on the evidence either of such sources as ancient Hindu texts or of those with clairvoyant sight. Developments in science within the last few decades have helped this aspect of our understanding, with the innovation of various high-voltage photographic techniques. These include Kirlian photography, which began in Russia in the mid-twentieth century: this is a method for producing still photographs of the energy field around any living thing. More recently, further techniques have been developed which are able to photograph, like a video or cine-film, the movement of these energy fields that are invisible to the average naked eye. These techniques show that the energy field of all living things extends way beyond the physical skin that we can see and touch: the part of the body that we see and feel is in fact the densest part of a much wider energy system which is in constant motion.

The Chakras

The "chakras" are wheels, or centres, which draw energy into the body from the universal energy field surrounding you. This energy is then distributed around the body via a network of pathways, known in acupuncture as meridians; and it radiates out into the "aura", which is the individual energy field surrounding you. The seven major chakras (there are many more, minor ones) radiate from seven points from the base of the spine to the top of the head (Fig. 1, p. 97). They have long been recognised in the East, therefore, by particular peoples and religions as the core of the system which sustains our life force. Plenty of information about the chakra system is available from other sources. What is relevant here is the correlation between these energy stations and the colours of the spectrum, from Red at the base to Violet at the crown.

The fact that, for thousands of years, Hindu and other ancient traditions have associated each of these energy centres with a rainbow hue, and each of these hues in turn with a particular area of the physical body, and of the aura, is the chief source of colour as a language. This is therefore important in your understanding of how and why colour has such a powerful practical bearing in your life.

The Aura

The word "aura" derives from Greek, in which it means, among other things, light. The aura is a living, moving, colourful field of energy that surrounds the physical body. It alters, in size and shape and colours, according to many factors such as your state of health, your age and activities, as well as your thoughts and feelings. Thus there is no single aura which is typical of all human beings. Fig. 2 (p. 98) is an idealised picture showing the several levels of the human aura as it could be in an unusually balanced state. Fig. 3 (p. 99) illustrates the aura of someone who is suffering mental illness and other ill health.

Though most people are not able to see these coloured fields of energy, there is nevertheless a level at which they have been perceived throughout time, and this is reflected universally, in every language on earth, in the phrases we use. It is from the largely unconscious recognition of this energy field that phrases such as *"feeling Blue"* or being *"in the Pink"*, and others, arise; because they refer to colour changes which take place within the aura when different states – of body, emotions, mind, or even spirit – prevail. This also accounts for the halo painted by artists throughout the ages to depict saints and other enlightened beings.

The aura is as vital an aspect of your physical life as is the body that you can see and touch. Edgar Cayce, whose exceptional gifts were used by many doctors because of the many miracle cures he achieved – often at a distance – through his clairvoyant sight, had seen auras from his earliest childhood. He discovered early in his life that when a person is marked for death the aura begins to fade, as the soul prepares itself to separate from the physical body. In a short essay on auras and colour that he wrote shortly before his death in 1945, he records the following anecdote, recounted to him by a friend with similar sight:

"One day in a large city I entered a department store to do some shopping. I was on the sixth floor and rang for the elevator. While I was waiting for it I noticed some bright red sweaters, and thought I would like to look at them. However, I had signaled for the elevator, and when it came I stepped forward to enter it. It was almost filled with people, but suddenly I was repelled. The interior of the car, although well-lighted, seemed dark to me. Something was wrong. Before I could analyze my action I said, 'Go ahead,' to the operator, and stepped back. I went over to look at the sweaters, and then I realized what had made me uneasy. The people in the elevator had no auras. While I was examining the sweaters, which had attracted me by their bright red hues – the color of vigor and energy – the elevator cable snapped, the car fell to the basement, and all the occupants were killed." (*Auras: An Essay on the Meaning of Colors*, Edgar Cayce, A.R.E. Press).

Founded largely on the association of the chakras with the various rainbow hues, there is a body of empirical knowledge which has been built up from the observation of human activity by mystics and healers, and sometimes by artists, since the time of the ancient Egyptians, and through many cultures. This has shown that every colour in the rainbow contains a wealth of information relating to us on a number of levels simultaneously: our bodies, our feelings and thoughts, and the deeper, more obscure aspects which are our soul or our consciousness. Colour can therefore act like a messenger, carrying the necessary information from cell to cell, which then respond in a way appropriate to that colour. Blue, for example, relates to the throat area; thus, while Blue applied around the neck may be helpful in soothing sore throats, the colour also applies to communication in a general sense. So the use of Blue, either applied physically or simply through the power of the message that it contains once you contemplate what it is that this colour reveals to you, will often empower your communications. It might do anything from helping a stammering child to polishing the performance of an actor on stage. Green relates to the heart area and thus not only to the circulation of energy in your body, but also to the flowing of emotions. Yellow applies to the solar plexus and the digestive organs, and its energy may help in the absorption of food or in the processing of information. Such attributes as these are general ones, relating to all mankind. The balancing of the different energy centres is fundamental to your well-being and harmony.

What is of even more central concern here is the personal, individual aspect of colour. You receive universal energy from the field around you, and you also radiate it. Part of what differentiates you from one another and forms your individuality is the *quality and hue* of this energy that you radiate. As you have seen, people have different vibrational rates, which contrast with one another, and this is reflected in the variety of their auras; or, in other words, of their *wavelengths*. It is at this level that colour is most vitally a reflection of your very essence. When you put attention into your conscious choice of the colour or colours that appeal most deeply to you, what is happening is that the colours you choose are, literally, *resonating* with this essential quality, which is your essence expressed through your dominant colours. In other words, when you recognise your truly favourite colours, you are, however unconsciously, recognising yourself!

Once you know a bit about what the various colours have to say, you can use this recognition when you make conscious selections of colour, to spot not only your own gifts and talents, and some of your limitations, but also the way in which these may interact with those around you. You can also, through using colour consciously, bring a new vitality to your positive qualities and modify some of the characteristics in you that have caused suffering and discomfort.

ENERGY EXCHANGE

Everything in our universe is energy in motion. This means, among other things, that in all your interactions with other people, in all your relationships of whatever nature, you are involved in an exchange of energy. This is easy to understand in a simple context. You visit, say, your car repair shop: the mechanic gives an hour of his time and skill (both of which translate to energy) to fix your car, and you pay him money (energy in a different form) in return. A simple swap. In personal relationships, this concept becomes less clear-cut, and a little harder to understand. Let's take an example.

Is there someone in your life – a neighbour, or a relative perhaps – who is especially needy? This may be someone who often comes to visit, or calls you on the phone. We will call her Jennifer. When you close the door after one of her visits, or finish another phone conversation, Jennifer obviously feels a lot better than she did half an hour ago; and *you feel wiped out*. Does this ring any bells? Or perhaps, at another time in your life, you might have needed someone else in a similar way? Now this is a much more complicated situation than the agreement with the man who repaired your car. That was a simple exchange of energy (money, in that case), in which both parties knew and understood the rules. Your encounter with Jennifer is also an exchange of energy; but here the exchange is uneven, and usually unconscious, and there are no rules: no clearly agreed terms such as you have with the car repair man. **To complicate things further, your auras have become merged**.

What lies behind this type of energy zapping in relationship is our need for energy. James Redfield has explained this phenomenon very thoroughly in *The Celestine Prophecy*. If you have not read this book, or have forgotten it, I would strongly recommend that you take a look at it. The phenomenon of energy zapping has to do with the fact that most of us have lost touch with the simple truth that supplies of energy are infinite, and that we can get all we need from the universe. Because we have lost touch with this truth, we are constantly wanting energy from other people. In a relationship with any personal content at all, it is inevitable that your aura plays a part: that you will be both giving and receiving energy through the aura in your interchange with the other person. When the exchange is a clear and positive one, all is well and good: both parties leave the encounter energised and buoyant. When there is less clarity in the equation, it is not quite so simple.

Let's look at another way in which this energy draining might work. Suppose you have a relative – we will call her Auntie Dorothy – who has always envied you because she has seen you as having talents and opportunities that she has not been given. Now this individual, rather than thanking you, as Jennifer did, on every occasion for making her feel so much better, may do exactly the opposite: each time she sees you, she may find subtle ways of putting you down, so that you come away with your confidence undermined and a vague feeling of depression. Just like Jennifer, the first type of person we suggested, *this person also leaves you drained.* The symptoms may feel different, but the cause is the same: she has made you feel worse so that she feels better. In other words, she has helped herself to your energy. She has, of course, no conscious idea that this is what she has done. And you have no conscious idea that this is what you have allowed. You could no doubt find countless other examples of this phenomenon: a boss who felt superior to you and remained aloof; a teacher who frightened you, and so on.

On the other hand, what about when you are in love? When you fall in love, you see everything in your world in the most positive way. This means that your energy field becomes as positive as it has ever been, and therefore very clear, so that you are in the best possible state to receive unlimited supplies of energy from the universe. The energy available from this universal source is infinite: the only thing preventing its free flow towards you is your own beliefs, which cause blockages, like a dam in a river. When you are fresh in the throes of love, your blockages will tend to evaporate. Energy simply pours through your aura and your veins. With this abundance of energy, it is the easiest thing in the world to give unlimited supplies of this to your loved one. This accounts for how you feel when you are in love, and for the glow you may sense around other couples who are in this state. You are each giving and receiving unlimited supplies of energy; so that you shine like the light bulbs which, for the time being, you are.

Wouldn't it be wonderful if you could experience such a state of joy and abundance as the norm? At present, there are very few people who are able to do so. The usual scenario is that, as the relationship progresses, little by little, you

> *Wouldn't it be wonderful if you could experience such a state of joy and abundance as the norm?*

will run up against some of the difficulties that we discussed in the last few chapters: the fear when you discover the differences between you, the discomfort when you encounter those aspects of yourself that you are unhappy about, and so on. The translucent glow of love may then start to turn into a series of battles – minor or major – with that very person with whom you may have hoped or decided to spend the rest of your life. **The power struggle has begun**.

A struggle for power is what happens when you fear that your needs are not being met by the person you are with. If, like most people, you have not learned to meet your own needs, you are likely to look to the person closest to you to meet them. There is one major catch in this arrangement: the odds are that this person is hoping for much the same deal from you! This process is largely unconscious. Even more unconscious is the fact that each of you is now beginning, instead of showering your loved one with ever-ready supplies of energy, to reverse that process and attempt to suck energy from the other one. Energy is synonymous with power. The bottom line is that power is energy; so what you are struggling for when you get locked into a battle for power is to ensure that you get enough energy!

You can analyse what is happening more accurately than just to say you are involved in a struggle for energy. The energy we are referring to is the universal life force – otherwise known as prana, or chi – which is the energy of light. And you have already seen that what happens as you receive this light is that it separates into different rays, which are related to different areas of your physiology and emotions, and also that you each resonate to a particular part of the spectrum, just as you have our own thumbprint or signature. So what happens in the energy exchange between two people is that you give or receive some colours more than others, depending on your nature, and on your circumstances, and on the personal issues you are dealing with.

My predominant colour is Magenta. When I first became involved in doing a lot of teaching, counselling and healing work, while I knew the theory, I often failed to notice what was actually happening to my energy as I worked with clients. It was not uncommon for me to wake up in the early morning as tired as when I had gone to bed, and with a craving for the colour Magenta so deep that I would have drunk even wine, had it been available, simply to satisfy my colour hunger. Once I replenished this colour through the application of Magenta-coloured lotions on my skin, or other methods (see Part Four), the craving would disappear and my energy would begin to return to normal. This direct, conscious correlation between a state of depletion and the necessary colour was probably brought about by the fact that I was working intensively with colour: in these situations energy is shifting at an accelerated pace, and one's sensitivities are therefore in a heightened state of awareness. There are plenty of other occasions in my life, as in everyone's, when tiredness of some sort cannot be so easily pinpointed and colour-coded. Nevertheless, the colour depletion is there, even when we are not aware of it.

In the same way, your needy friend or relation may lock into an area where you are strong, and unwittingly help herself to generous portions of your Turquoise energy, say, or your Gold. As you learn, through your colour choices, to understand your own true colours – your weaknesses along with your strengths – you will gradually take back the control of your energy field. You will learn to give back all the energy that does not belong to you, and that perhaps does not harmonise with or enhance your own (Auntie Dorothy's, for example); and you will learn to reclaim all that energy which is your own (from both Auntie Dorothy and Jennifer). You can then *choose* to offer power, *consciously*, to a friend or partner. The way you can do this is to give that person your real attention: by being fully in the moment with another person, you can not only listen with attention, but you can also speak your truth. When your communication becomes conscious, you are both able to offer power consciously to one another: in this way, neither party becomes drained. In intimate relationship above all others, it is essential that this process is understood.

 1 *A power struggle is the quickest road to mutual depletion, and*
 2 *The conscious offering of power to one another through loving support*
  is the best road to mutual strength.

Once you have learned to control your energy field, so that you feel abundant as well as clear, everybody wins: the power struggle will cease as you, along with your partner, take back your power and regain the strength that you had given away. The underlying truth is that you probably began to lose that autonomy so long ago, in childhood, that you never knew you had been in possession of it in the first place. The "falling in love" episode, which most people have experienced at one time or another, was actually a reminder of that integrity and fullness that was your original state. When you lose something, it is so that you have to work to find it again; and what you work for has a new value and completeness because of the effort you have put in. So when you re-gain your power it is with a new integrity, and certainty, and force. In this state of abundance, you are both in a position to give energy consciously to each other; to nurture and be nurtured; to listen and be heard; to see and be seen.

PART TWO

WHAT COLOUR ARE YOU? WHAT COLOUR AM I?

And Life is Colour and Warmth and Light
And a striving evermore for these.

JULIAN GRENFELL
INTO BATTLE 1915

chapter 4

RECOGNISING YOURSELF

This above all: to thine own self be true,
And it must follow, as the night the day,
Thou canst not then be false to any man.

Shakespeare

Hamlet

W hat do the various colours offered in this book have to teach? And how can you bring the use of colour into helping you along with your relationships? A simple experience will pave the way here for you to experience colour in a new way. Fig. 4 (pp. 100–1) shows you a range of different spectrum colours, and inside the front and back cover of the book you will find the cut-out colour cards which were mentioned in Chapter 1. Cut these out and arrange them however you like, preferably against a background of White or neutral. Contemplate the colours for a while. If you are working with a partner, then contemplate them together. Then, each choose the one colour card that attracts you the most; the colour that you will happily live with for some time to come. Think about this colour.

- *Does it have any particular associations for you?*
- *Does it make you feel happy or sad, warm or cold?*
- *Does it excite you and stimulate you into action, or does it make you feel relaxed and quiet?*
- *Would you like to wear it in your clothes or sleep with it in your sheets?*
- *Would you prefer to see just a little of it in your ornaments and pictures, or in the flowers in your garden or house plants?*
- *Would you like to include it in your furnishings or paint it on to your walls?*

- *Have you always been aware of this colour as one that draws you, or does it surprise you to find that you like it?*
- *Close your eyes and allow the colour to flow around in your mind.*

Now write down all the things that come to mind in relation to this colour. Try to describe the feelings in you that the colour evokes.

Take a trip around your home. Whether home is a bed-sit or a mansion, look at the details. Look inside your wardrobe and see what colours are there. Do you have a large cross-section, or is your selection limited to a few oft-repeated hues? Look around you and see what different colours strike you in your living space. Do you have plenty of colours? Or could this space do with a lift? Later, you will select more colours from these spectrum cards.

Paying Attention to Colour

Whether you live in the sunny south or the frozen north, the first discovery you need to make in working with colour is your own particular preferences. As you read through the next few chapters, you may find that you begin to notice the ways in which the colours you choose might feature in your daily living. Invite these colours gently into your life: above all, into your thoughts and your feelings; but also into the material details of your daily living. If you buy a bunch of flowers, some bath bubbles or a bar of soap, remember to colour-code your choice.

A good preparation for working with colour is simply to start to pay attention, though in Part Four you will find specific methods through which colour can be made available to you, to include such things as not only the colour of the clothes you wear and the foods you eat, but also the possibility of using other media such as coloured oils, coloured crystals, coloured baths, or the visualisation of colour. When you get up in the mornings, notice which colour you would like to have around you today. You will probably find that as you open to the possibility of receiving more colours than you have done before, new colours will present themselves to you. A good Japanese housewife does her best to offer her family 38 different foodstuffs each day, on the basis that a thoroughly varied diet promotes optimum health. You would do well to take a leaf out of her book and apply the principle not only to your diet but also to the colours you put around you in your surroundings and your daily routine. This is because not only does each person have a small number of colours that relate specifically to their essential quality, and which can therefore serve simultaneously as a diagnostic tool and a personal remedy. Each person also needs a variety of colours around them, in order to nourish the different energy centres and achieve optimum balance and health.

The next few chapters will introduce you to the language of colour, so that you can begin to understand the messages within those colours that particularly attract you. The "personality sketches" for a number of commonly used colours will show you the possibility of recognising, and understanding better, aspects of yourself and your friends, through the colours you and they choose. Colour is merely a mirror. It offers no judgment of any sort. This is a useful reminder when you set out to work on the quality of your relationships, when the first thing you need to let go of is judgment, both of yourself and of each other. Once you stop justifying, making excuses, judging yourself or blaming each other, you can begin to see, enjoy and work with what *is*.

Colour in Communication

When you come to contemplate colour with the intention of deciding which are those hues that appeal to you the most, on a more permanent basis than just the choice of this season's shirt, you can then harness the language of colour to access an understanding of your thoughts and emotions which goes much deeper than just the mood of the moment. Similarly, the contemplation of some of the inner meaning of colour can lead you towards an understanding of the ways in which you unconsciously "speak" to one another. Colour offers you the compassion, and hands you the power, to dispense with pretence and get real in your connection with *yourself*, and so it enables you also to make contact with each other. Here is a raw material as old as time itself – colour and light – but which can be fashioned into a new tool for the deepening and enrichment of that part of your life without which all the diamonds and rubies in the world would be worthless: the intimate friendships you share with the people you love. The spirit of our communication affects everything, from half an hour spent in sharing a meal with a friend to the years of wars that sacrifice thousands of lives. Relationship is about communication; and the art of true communication is as vital to our personal fulfilment as it is, ultimately, to the survival of the human race. Colour and light show us how to make that communication more conscious, and therefore to use this gift creatively to become masters of our destiny rather than victims of our experience.

This is where the fun really begins. Every colour has its own personality, so to speak, which tells you much about the people choosing it – especially yourself and those close to you. Each colour also relates to other colours in particular ways. When you understand something of these interactions, then suddenly you see why your mother-in-law – or someone even closer to home – has driven you mad all these years. Life is a process of perpetual movement – inner and outer – within and around relationship. Whether you like it or not, you are both a product of your earlier kinships and a function of your current ones. Relationship is not an optional extra. Life *is* relationship, as everyday you interact with a lover or spouse, a parent, a son or daughter, an employer or an employee, a teacher or pupil; whatever.

The common denominator in all these relationships is yourself; and colour and light offer you, in the gentlest way possible, the opportunity to see yourself without the illusions that bar your way to honesty and truth. From this place, you can let go of self-deception and begin to recognise the completeness, the complexity – and the power – of what you are. Relationship begins at home, in other words, in the way you connect with yourself. This involves the shedding of illusion so that you can unlock your shackles and recognise the full package of who you are, acknowledging your weaknesses but also – and this is even more important – discovering your strengths. **This is the route to freedom**.

Just as every person has strengths and weaknesses, so each colour shows aspects that may be seen as gifts and others that are more likely to appear as hurdles to be overcome. We all have a few devils inside us as well as angels. Or it may be that – as you saw briefly in Chapter 3 in cases of accident, shock or illness – these colour choices alert you to areas of depletion where that colour is *needed*. In recognising yourself, you can allow your colours to empower you; and you can also allow them to show you those areas which need shaping up a bit. The difficulties your choices present, reflected by the colours that you and no-one else have selected, are merely the difficulties your higher, or unconscious, self recognises as those which have not only held you back in the past, but which also contain the potential for huge growth, once they are turned around. You can work with and through these challenges, just as you can work with and through the difficulties with one another, and so transmute them, through understanding, into some of your greatest strengths.

chapter 5

PRIMARY COLOURS

Colors are the children of light, and light is their mother.

Johannes Itten

The Elements of Color

I f you are anxious to get on and investigate the meaning of your own colour selection, you may wish to pick out from these next three chapters only those colours that have an immediate bearing on your own selection, or on your joint selection as a couple. Unlike most of the other parts in this book, these next few pages are quite theoretical. However, there is one reason in particular, if you have a head for any theory, why it is helpful to look at the information contained here. This is the fact that every colour that you choose, whether from this book or anywhere else in the world, has a vital relationship with one or more of the primary colours; so that an understanding of the basic nature of these three essential hues provides a strong foundation for everything that follows. This foundation will give you a deeper understanding and feel for the individual colours you choose.

The language of colour could be described as a character-mapping tool, which has been derived mainly from our historical and empirical knowledge. It was briefly explained in Chapter 3 that through many centuries of observation, mystics, artists and those practising colour therapy have, drop by drop, created a well of information around each of these primary and other colours, which offers insights on several levels, including even the physical. It is useful also to appreciate the origins and basis of colour from the standpoint of science. These two perspectives together offer a fairly comprehensive understanding of colour as a vehicle for connecting with many of the emotional, psychological and spiritual aspects of humanity, which are what is most helpful in looking at the gifts and challenges presented in our relationships with one another.

THE SPECTRUM

Colour is the visible part of the whole of the electromagnetic spectrum of White light. Any person with normal vision can perceive within the rainbow, or visible spectrum, the three colours appearing at intervals within it from which all the other colours may be obtained. These are the three primary colours, Red, Blue and Yellow. Between these are the secondary ones, Green, Orange and Violet. For the benefit of those readers who are concerned with the scientific understanding of colour, it is necessary to state here that there are slightly (though not significantly) different schools of thought within colour theory: these apply mainly to the definition of complementary pairs of colours. The understanding of colour relationships is further complicated by the fact that colours behave differently according to whether they are combined in light or in pigment. The insights offered in this and subsequent chapters are based upon the way in which colours act and interact when combined in pigment rather than light. Standard colour printers for home use obtain their spectrum of colours from the three main primaries which will be discussed here: Red, Blue and Yellow. Laser printers used commercially are able to produce very high quality colour reproduction through a more subtle mix of Yellow, Cyan (a type of Blue), Magenta (near to Red) and Black, which by bringing in the possibility of darker and lighter shades allows for more accurate colour resolution. Pictures produced upon a screen, on the other hand, are arrived at through a different combination of primary colours. This is because these pictures come from colour expressed directly through light rather than through pigment. This process is known as additive colour mixing: the method is to project Red, Green and Blue lights on to a White surface. This method is not relevant to this text.

The spectrum of colours, from Red through to Violet, originally analysed by Sir Isaac Newton in the late 1600s, can easily be assembled in such a way as to show how colours behave when combined together in pigment. The formation of a colour wheel or circle by mixing coloured paints is known as subtractive colour mixing. This has been done in a number of different ways, ever since Newton first constructed a wheel from the seven colours of the spectrum. One of the simplest methods is to draw a circle around an equilateral triangle containing the three primary colours, and then to extend it, forming a full wheel which incorporates all of the three primary colours, Red, Blue and Yellow, and all their intermediaries. Figs. 6–8 (pp. 103–4) illustrate the formation of this wheel.

The primary colours are the starting point for any investigation into colour. It is from different combinations of these three colours – Red, Blue and Yellow – that all other colours are derived. Conversely, they themselves cannot be derived from any other colours. This means that the primary colours have a **clarity** and **straightforwardness** of character: Blue, for example, can only be Blue; it contains no Yellow and no Red. By the same token, Yellow can only be Yellow and Red can only be Red. Colour "therapy", of any sort, is based upon the resonance of any particular colour with the person choosing it. While everyone resonates with a number of different colours, there are nevertheless predominant tendencies in all of us. The character of a colour, therefore, is also a reflection of the character of the person choosing it. You may be more of a "Red" person than a "Yellow" or a "Blue" one. In the descriptions of colours that follow, the reference to any colour often refers to a person, rather as a homoeopathic remedy describes the essential qualities of the person choosing it, or an astrological sign describes the nature of a person born under its influence.

The visible spectrum of colour can be looked at from a few different perspectives, each of which offers clues to the meanings of all the spectrum colours, and – in the context of this chapter – of the three primary colours in particular. Fig. 5 (p. 102) brings most of these perspectives together in one diagram. These perspectives, briefly summarised below, provide some simple tools for gaining a fundamental grasp of the nature of Red, Blue and Yellow.

Cool or Hot? – Fast or Slow?

Fig. 5 (p. 102) illustrates the spectrum of light that comes from the sun, and shows where the visible colours fit into this spectrum. The rays towards the Red end of the spectrum are hotter than those at the other end. **Red**, in other words, is a "**hot**" ray; **Blue** is a "**cool**" one. This concept applies to us in what might be described as ways both outer and inner. On the one hand, it influences our use of colour (do you like, for instance, to feel cool in a Blue bathroom, or do you prefer to be surrounded when naked by something a little more stimulating to the circulation?). On the other hand – and this is more relevant in the context of this book – it applies to the character of a person predominantly drawn to one or other end of the spectrum: in other words, whether you are "hot-headed" or "cool as a cucumber" is likely to be reflected within your choice of colours. The remaining primary colour, **Yellow**, comes between the two extremes: it is neither too hot nor too cool.

Stimulating or Calming?

You will also see something else: at the Red end of the spectrum the wavelengths are long and slow; and at the Blue (and Violet) end they are short and fast. This means that, although the Red wavelength is slow, its sheer size gives it strength: like the ocean wave, **Red** is **powerful** and **stimulating**. Blue, on the other hand, nearer to the Violet end of the spectrum, has a wavelength which is shorter and faster. This means that the effect of **Blue**, and of the other colours at this end of the spectrum, is **calming** and **soothing**. This is evidenced in the use of ultra-Violet rays for calming cancerous overgrowths. In this context, too, **Yellow** comes somewhere in the middle; near the centre of the body, this colour plays a key role in the **assimilation** of both energy and knowledge.

On Earth or in Heaven?

Fig. 5 (p. 102) illustrates the chakras as part of the source from where the meanings of colours have come to be understood. The traditional Hindu view of the connection between the spectrum colours and the chakras in the body places **Red** at the base, connecting us with the **earth**, and ascending through the energy stations to the **Blue** (and Violet) range of colours around the neck and head, which connect us with the **sky or heaven**. **Yellow**, occupying its usual position in between the two extremes, stands for the **individual** poised between heaven and earth.

Pulling or Pushing?

Another clue about the nature of two of the primary colours comes from astronomy. In astronomy, **Blue** is perceived as the colour radiated by approaching galaxies, whereas **Red** is emitted by those galaxies that are moving away from us. This tells us a certain amount about the fundamental quality of these two rays: Blue is associated with a tendency towards **introversion** and **acquisition**; to attract energy towards us and to look inward. Red, on the other hand, is associated with an extrovert nature: the tendency to **push** our energy and focus our attention **outwards**; this can cause a "Red" person to **reject** experience. Aura-Soma colour theory has further understood and developed this concept (and also drawn upon ancient Buddhist philosophy), to explain Yellow as a colour that is between these two extremes: **Yellow** does not always know whether it is coming or going, and can therefore be **confused**.

• • • • •

It is our personal choice of colour that reflects our resonance with any particular wavelength of light. In applying these colour traits to a human personality, it is easy to begin to sketch a portrait of the Red, Or Blue, or Yellow character. The **Red** personality, for instance, can be briefly summarised from the perspectives just offered as: hot, slow though powerful (like an ocean wave, for example), stimulating, well connected with the earth, and having a tendency to push outwards. Here is a summary of these fundamental characteristics of the three primary colours:

Red	Blue	Yellow
Hot	Cool	Warm
Slow	Fast	Moderate
Stimulates	Calms	Assimilates
"Feet on earth"	"Head in Heaven"	Individualist
Rejects	Acquires	Confused

Some people are drawn towards the simplicity and directness of the primary colours. Whether you are or not, these basic hues are contained, in a hidden form, within any of the colours you select. This is why it is helpful to get to know them a little. The descriptions that follow will present both strengths and difficulties in every colour. Within any of the energy centres – and therefore colour stations – of the body, we have the potential to move out of the ideal state of equilibrium. There may be either too much or too little of that ray within our aura; and this is what is meant when the text refers to an **imbalance**. An overdose or an under-supply is likely to give rise to difficulties, as will be apparent from the descriptions of the colours.

Key words and concepts are presented in bold type, for easy reference and also to help you to fix them in your mind. The genders attributed to each description will alternate, generally between paragraphs. This is deliberate, in order to avoid the pitfall of implying that any colour is weighted towards either end of the gender scale. **Please note**, however, that all of the characteristics ascribed to any particular colour apply equally to people of both sexes, even though the paragraph may make reference to one or other gender. Neither does it matter where we begin in this trilogy of primary colours. We were all children once upon a time; and most children love the colour Red. Here is as good a starting point as any other. We shall then work clockwise around the colour wheel, through this and subsequent chapters.

RED

Red relates to our connection with the **earth**. It is a primary colour: in other words, in its pure form, the Red hue contains no Yellow and no Blue. The simplicity and straightforwardness that characterises the primary colours means that while the person strongly drawn towards the colour Red may sometimes lack subtlety, he is also likely to be quite clear and direct. The "Red" person is generally **strong** and **active**, and enjoys the physical and material aspects of life. The colour Red has a fiery strength, and it symbolises both vitalised earth and the vitality carried by our own **blood** in circulation. This person tends to have a strong sense of **commitment** to, and even **passion** for, whatever engages his attention and energy. He is the **extrovert**, always going out to meet the world, even though such a meeting may often be on his own terms.

The light emitted by receding galaxies is towards the Red end of the spectrum; so the 'Red' person is inclined to project his energy outwards, pushing out rather than pulling in. This tendency may apply to many aspects of Red's experience, including of course his interactions with those around him. In his anxiety to push away whatever it is that he may find threatening in some way, Red has a tendency to give his power away by **reacting** strongly against whatever it is that he does not like. By doing this, he gives more energy to those things that he wants to reject, making it more likely that, whatever they are, they will bounce back to him, like a ball on a squash court. One of his lessons is to learn to stand back and find the **detachment** necessary to weigh up a situation before he jumps in with both feet and gets damaged (or causes damage!), which he tends to do over and over again, especially as his memory span is short and he will easily forget what happened the last time…. Not being someone given to introspection, Red has extrovert habits that can serve as a powerful tool for avoiding close personal encounters. He tends to be **solid**, **stable** and **well-grounded**. He is **impulsive**, **enthusiastic**, and quite probably **impatient**.

Preferring action to reflection, this is someone who is more likely to be successful as a business person than as a philosopher. She is more interested in the "how" than the "why". Drawn to practice rather than to theory, she is also literal rather than poetic. This may render her, from time to time, a little heavy-footed and obtuse; even **tactless**. Her impulsiveness can be extreme: she throws caution to the winds, hurling herself into all manner of deep ends before she has learned to swim; this may cause shock and even exasperation to her more cautious family and friends. They recognise, however, the vital role she plays in all their lives, and they may sometimes envy her **initiative** and **strength**. Though she can be **selfish** and demanding at times, she is also **generous**, **passionate** and very **loving**. She will readily concern herself with issues of **material survival**, and she will enjoy the resulting comfort and security of wealth; but she is also capable, when the situation demands it, of the greatest acts of **self-sacrifice**. The **courage** and **daring** which are a part of the Red person's strength may well combine with her essentially **practical** nature to make her something of an **innovator**.

A strong liking for Red, as with any colour, may alert us to some of its more difficult aspects. Red is the colour of energy and physicality, yet the choice of it may indicate someone who is in great need of **physical energy**; someone who, tired out, lacks the commitment or courage to take hold of the reins in their life, or to say no when necessary. It can suggest anxiety around money and survival. It may also show that there are powerful emotions such as **anger**, **frustration** or resentment which need to be expressed. Red sometimes indicates **violence**, emotional or physical, towards others or oneself. The tendency in Red towards impulsive reactions may sometimes combine with the powerful Red emotions to produce someone who quite quickly loses control of her temper; but she lives in the **present** and the future rather than in the past: she will bear no grudges as she rushes on to the next thing. Her bark is much worse than her bite and she may well be oblivious of any hurt that her outburst has caused. Just as Red paint on objects such as cars fades more quickly than many other colours, so it is with Red's nature. This is the **sprinter** rather than the long-distance runner. Though capable of the most powerful commitment, she often works in short sharp bursts of energy rather than at a steady pace.

Though Red is often enterprising and energetic, beware! – he is capable, too, of a **stubbornness** as dogged as any mule. The colour Red has the slowest wavelength in the visible spectrum of light; it is also the most **stimulating** one. This Red power is that of the ocean wave, which relentlessly pursues its course. Tuned in, as the Red person is, to the denser vibrations and therefore reluctant to change his mind once he is set upon a direction, Red may also allow himself from time to time to become so earth-bound that he might be described as a stick-in-the-mud.

In health, the Red person is **bountiful, spontaneous, warm-blooded** in every sense, and full of love. He is very loving and very loveable. He may not look before he leaps; he may burn his fingers from time to time, and he may sometimes hurt others. But he lives in the present; he is the eternal **optimist** and loves experiment. He is **versatile** and perpetually **resourceful**; his mistakes will never stop him from trying again.

> ### RED AFFIRMATION
> *I am grateful for my health and my life.*
> *Each new day is a gift which I greet with*
> *vitality and passion.*

A note about the Paler Colours

The paler colours in general are known as **tints**. In colour therapy, these paler tints are generally seen as being more intense than the deeper hues, rather than less so, which is different from the conventional view of the deeper colours as being stronger. They are more intense, or potent, because they contain more White, or more light: this means that, while on the one hand they may indicate an urgency around the issues they bring to our attention – e.g. extreme concerns around the issue of survival or an extreme need for love – there is also the probability that some of the difficulties within this ray have already been seen and recognised, and even overcome. This would then lead to a different kind of intensity: in the "Pale Red" ray, which of course is Pink, an extreme generosity, absolute love and the readiness to sacrifice oneself for the sake of another.

There is no colour known as Pale Red, for once Red becomes pale – in other words once it is combined with White – it changes its name to Pink. This is significant because these two colours – Red and Pink – have a lot in common; and yet they are also quite distinct from each other. Pink is included in this chapter because, technically, it is as near to being a primary colour as Pale Blue and Pale Yellow are, although all these might be better described from a visual stance as "primary pastels".

PINK

Like Red, Pink has a lot to do with **love, generosity** and **warmth**. The quality of this energy, however, is very different from that of Red. This colour brings White into the strong primary quality of the Red, creating an energy which is softer than either of these "parent" hues. Where Red is passionate and enthusiastic, and can demand active love in return for all she offers, the Pink quality is softer. Where Red is passion, Pink is **compassion**. Where Red love may be conditional, Pink loves without terms or limitations. Someone drawn to Pink is likely to be a very **sensitive, intuitive** individual who offers strong and gentle support to those close to her. If she is wise, she will trust her inner voice: the still small voice of instinct is her surest guide. This intuition is a powerful tool in her work and in her personal life.

The tenderness and sensitivity of the Pink can also be its greatest difficulty. The person who chooses a lot of Pink may be highly **vulnerable**. The slightest touch, to this person, may be experienced as a bruise. **Generous** to a fault, this person may give and give to everyone but himself, and then wonder why he is exhausted. He finds it easy to give; his lesson may be in learning to **receive**. It may be that, in the past, he has felt his hold on life and love to be only a tenuous one, where he must constantly be giving to others in order to obtain the love that he has needed.

The Pink person may feel **insubstantial**: Pink and frothy and sugar-sweet, but empty inside. She may suffer from a lack of courage and commitment in her life. This person may have suffered the consequences of being **unable to say "no"**. She may feel the need always to show kindness on the outside, so as to please those around her, while in fact she is harbouring deeply hidden anger and resentment. This inability to express her real emotions might account for the tendency in Pink towards **sentimentality** rather than real feeling. These difficulties have their origin in the secret which lies hidden within the Pink energy: the colour Red, which combined with White to create this colour. Pink may contain within her depths not only concealed anger and frustration, and perhaps a vulnerability so deep that even her survival feels itself to be on the line, but also a subtler form of passion.

This colour relates to the **feminine** aspect of our nature. A man or woman strongly drawn to Pink is likely to be in touch with their own intuitive, creative aspect. **Sensitive**, **tender**, **loving** and **kind**, they may, too, suffer from difficulties with the **mother-role** and, above all, with getting their own needs met while over-caring for those around them. The simple law that we cannot give what we do not have contains a lesson that applies most particularly to those who are strongly drawn to the colour Pink. One of the consequences of this characteristic of the Pink person, in imbalance, is that they may find it very **hard to grow up**.

There can be a strength as well as a passion hidden within the Pink, which is not immediately apparent to those who only notice her kindness and warmth. This has its source in the power of **unconditional love**: this person, in health, has a nature which **accepts** and **supports** things exactly the way they are; she **forgives** readily and is not easily overcome by the desire to control or alter those around her. This passionate strength means that she will protect those in her care with the ferocity, if necessary, of a lioness: once given, the commitment in Pink is **selfless** and total. When the difficulties around self-nurturing and self-respect can be overcome, the gifts in the Pink are manifold: a bottomless well of **unconditional love**, **imagination**, **creativity**, **tenderness** and **compassion**.

Pale pink

Pale Pink contains everything that is already within the colour Pink, but in the most intense form. The person drawn to this tint is generally someone of very great sensitivity and warmth, and absolute generosity; she is someone who gives without the slightest thought for the cost. She is extremely tender; extremely compassionate. Her intuition is probably highly developed, and it is this, above all, that gives rise to her creative gifts. With all these qualities, she is nevertheless very vulnerable: it may be high time that this person learned how to say no, how to protect herself, and how to cultivate a few of her own needs and desires before she finds herself quite washed out. So long as she does this, Pale Pink will enjoy the companionship and warmth that are freely returned to her by those to whom she is so open and giving.

> ## PINK AFFIRMATION
> *I am ready and willing to receive all the love that is waiting for me; I love and accept myself just the way I am.*

BLUE

At the opposite end of the spectrum from Red, Blue is a **cool** ray. Like a clear summer sky, it offers a sense of **peace**. The person who chooses Blue is, or at least has the capacity to be, a peaceful communicator. Like all primary colours, Blue emanates a straightforward quality of clarity and strength. She has a well-developed sense of **independence** and tends to radiate a feeling of **authority, solidity** and **stillness**. In a well-balanced state, she has no need to go out and meet the world, as this stillness within her attracts those around her, just as birds are attracted to the still, strong branches of a tree. The Blue person has a natural sense of **protectiveness** towards those around her, so that others come very easily to rely upon this person. Just as Red is always active in a physical and material sense, Blue is, in this sense, passive. The Blue person, while quietly **authoritative**, is also **private** and **introverted**. Remember that the light from a star moving at high speed towards us is biased towards the Blue. By the same token, the person strongly drawn towards the colour Blue is likely to be **receptive**, perhaps **acquisitive**, and given to introspection. Being of a reflective, contemplative nature, she has the capacity – once she learns to use it – for clear **speaking** and also for attentive **listening**. She has the potential to be highly articulate in the communication of her thoughts; her feelings, however, she is more likely to keep to herself.

Blue is passive in a physical sense; but in a spiritual sense, this is among the most active rays. The Blue sky relates to heaven, and the person who often chooses Blue may sometimes find it hard to be **practical** and **realistic**, unconsciously preferring heaven to earth. It is likely that he will have a need to develop the spiritual aspect of his nature. He wants peace and tranquillity, too, for those he cares about; so he is very protective of those close to him, which is part of his strength. But there are times when his need for peace can become unbalanced, so that he will go out of his way to avoid any kind of confrontation in the hope of **peace at any price**. This shows that he may have a difficulty in claiming his autonomy and power. In health, the Blue person has a strong sense of **discipline** and power; in imbalance, he may show a resistance to **authority**, or the resentment of it, which in turn leads to, or may stem from, a problem in taking responsibility for himself. Blue relates predominantly to the **masculine** side of our nature. The choice of a lot of Blue may indicate that there have been **difficulties with the father** and that it is this which has led to subsequent problems around the issue of the "male", and around authority in general.

The "true Blue" person often tends towards **conservatism** in many areas of his life. He may prefer his old Blue jumper to his new Christmas present; he may dislike foreign food, and resent the various changes that inevitably come into his life. Without a clear **structure** Blue may well feel insecure. **Protective** of others, he also likes to feel protected and safe, and challenges to his way of life and ideas may well present themselves as threats to his sense of security. He is also prone to feeling Blue; in other words, he may well suffer frequent bouts of **depression**, or at least despondency. While he has a need for privacy, he may also suffer **loneliness** and isolation. Like the novelist, he has developed his powers of **observation**; but the one who always observes sometimes wishes for greater participation. The Blue person is more likely to be a loner than a regular part of a crowd.

The Blue person, in a state of harmony, has a strong sense of **service**, and of **divinity**. She has high **ideals** and **principles**, and she has begun to learn the lessons of **patience**, and of living in the present. When Blue overcomes her tendency to hold on, for the sake of **security**, to whatever she already possesses and knows, she will discover the **faith, acceptance**, and **trust** in the process of life which offers the ultimate, rare gift: **peace of mind**. Blue's Achilles' heel, however, is this very proclivity to take in and hold on, to grasp and cling in the hope of finding security. Blue people often find it hard to let go. When we understand where this Blue tendency is coming from, there is the possibility of transmuting this quality from something of a handicap to a great strength: the peace of mind that comes when we have discovered a real sense of **faith** and **trust**.

Pale Blue

The intense form of the Blue, this colour suggests all that is associated with Blue, together with the possibility of **stillness**, faith and a sense of trust. This is someone who, although he may at times feel extremely alone, nevertheless has a fundamental acceptance of a higher will, the universal mind, or however it is that he may understand the concept of source or divinity. While he may have suffered in the past over issues of nurturing and security, he has probably now recognised that he has always received what he has needed in the past, and therefore he worries less about the future. While he may once have grappled with difficulties over the question of authority, he is secure, now, in his own autonomy. The demands of his ego are substantially overcome, so that he may now be able to say – knowing that this is the true route to inner peace – "I trust that whatever each moment brings is for my highest good."

> *BLUE AFFIRMATION*
> *As I protect others, so I am protected. Like the Blue of a clear sky on a summer's day, I feel and breathe serenity and peace.*

YELLOW

Yellow is all **sunshine**, **radiance** and **laughter**. The colour relates to the third, or solar plexus, chakra, which is located just above the navel at the "sun centre" of the body. Like Red, Yellow contains a natural purity and frankness. Its primary nature gives it a quality of **sharpness**. Children's paintings generally portray the sun as a sphere of Yellow appearing in a Blue sky. The sun actually emits full-spectrum White light, but we perceive this (as we perceive light bulbs) as Yellow. Yellow is the most light-giving of all the hues, and those choosing it tend towards a **light**, **sunny** personality. The Yellow person is likely to be **"bright"**; in other words she has a **lively intellect**. She has the capacity, through sharp incisive thinking, to "see the light" of a truth which has been previously hidden.

Her **intellect** and her capacity for rational thought are powerful tools. The Yellow person also has a **strong will** which can be a great ally when well used. This is the person who knows that we can achieve anything if we put the force of our will behind it. Always busy with a new project or a new idea, she is not given to sitting around. **Active** and **alert**, she keeps her ear to the ground and tends to be keenly observant of all that is going on around her. She is an **individualist** and may on occasion be an **egotist**. In health, this person has accessed her **personal power** and has a balanced sense of her own value. She knows and trusts her intellect and tends to make up her own mind about things, not caring a great deal what others think.

When the Yellow energy has not been fully awakened and harmonised, the choice of it — as with other colours — may indicate a state of **need** rather than fullness. Where the Blue tendency is to acquire and hold on to what life offers, and the Red tendency is to react strongly and push experience away, Yellow is caught in the middle. His problem can be the most agonising **doubt** and **confusion**, and his suffering comes from not knowing what he wants. His strength, on the other hand, is precisely the other side of this coin: Yellow, once he has accepted his own confusion, is able to confront it and emerge with a **clarity** which is all the greater for the soul-searching, unwelcome though this may have been.

Yellow, like the other primary colours, has strengths that are powerful, and weaknesses to match: in her unbalanced state, this may result in **selfishness**, **falseness**, **greed** and **unreason**; or as a complete lack of **self-confidence**. Another caution, within the tendency towards egotism in the Yellow, is not to allow the force of the intellect either to lead you into **cynicism** or the destructiveness of **sarcasm**, or to dominate and suppress the voice of feeling.

The path of the person predominantly drawn to Yellow is eased by his ever-ready **sense of humour**. He can, even in quite extreme situations, nearly always recognise the absurdity of a predicament and make others laugh. When he gets stressed out, wound up with **anxiety** and **tension**, he is relatively easy to help: where others might need a good cry, the Yellow person will find a better release through laughter. His nature is fundamentally a **happy** one. Like the Gold person, however, he may have difficulty in absorbing the hard lessons of experience; in which case, he may become **fearful** and confused. The fear that can overwhelm him may lead sometimes to "Yellow-bellied" acts of **cowardice**.

The Yellow person, whether he works in the courts of law or on a building site, whether he is the student or the teacher, is **on the ball** and wide awake. He may be **highly strung**, and he must be careful not to abuse power; but he has the capacity to bring sunshine and laughter into the lives of all those around him, as well as into his own: like the great pianist, Arthur Rubinstein, the Yellow individual may well justify the claim that "I am the happiest man I've ever met".

Pale Yellow

All that is contained within the Yellow is also within this colour, and those characteristics which it indicates tend to be experienced here in a more intense form. In common with the other paler hues, the intensity in this colour comes from the fact that it incorporates a degree of White, which itself suggests light, understanding and clarity. This colour is often chosen to indicate a path of some suffering that has brought a person to this point where he sees an issue more clearly than before. Pale Yellow, while it may suggest some **intense fear** and confusion, also contains the promise of **sharp clarity**. The Yellow person is **quick-witted** and **clear-sighted**. He may not suffer fools gladly, and is certainly not easily fooled. Nor would he tolerate situations that bore him, but he is probably well able to avoid them. Perhaps above all, the gift within the person choosing this ray, apart from clarity of thought, wit, humour and the possibility of great happiness, is the potential for a rare degree of **self-knowledge**, which in turn leads him to a good understanding of mankind in general.

YELLOW AFFIRMATION

I am love and light; through the power of sunshine I dissolve all fears and confusion, and bring joy to all that I do.

• • • • •

These are some of the main features associated with the primary colours. When you come to choose the colours that draw you the most, and later to analyse your full selection, it is helpful to notice whether your overall selection leans towards one or another of these hues. In the next chapter, we shall look at the secondary colours, which combine the characteristics of two primaries and are a little more complex and subtle. They contain the energies of the colours from which they are made up, and then add to this a flavour of their own.

chapter 6

SECONDARY COLOURS

Rain, rain and sun! a rainbow in the sky!
A young man will be wiser by and by;

Tennyson

The Passing of Arthur

The colour wheel, or circle (Fig. 7–8, pp. 103–4), which was introduced in the last chapter, becomes useful as you go on to look at secondary colours. The wheel shows the three primary colours, Red and Blue and Yellow, and their intermediaries: these are the three secondary colours Green and Orange and Violet, and the six tertiary colours Magenta, Indigo, Turquoise, Olive Green, Gold and Coral. In this circle, each primary colour appears directly opposite to a secondary one. And, the wheel shows that, in each case, the secondary colour opposite to any primary colour is comprised of the remaining two primary colours. Yellow, for example, appears opposite the secondary colour Violet, which in turn is composed of the two primary colours, Red and Blue.

Blue + Orange = Blue + (Yellow + Red)

Red + Green = Red + (Yellow + Blue)

Yellow + Violet = Yellow + (Red + Blue)

The secondary colours, combining the characteristics of two primaries, are a little more **complex** and **subtle** than their parent hues. When the primary colours combine together to produce secondary hues, these combinations contain something of the qualities of the original rays, and they also bring their own particular character. Orange, for example, has its own distinctive and recognisable character, and it also reflects aspects of both the Red and the Yellow that it contains; so that the resulting colour has a greater complexity than the colours from which it originates. This is not a value judgment: no colour has a greater intrinsic worth than any other. Greater subtlety and complexity may also contain, for example and among many other things, less certainty and more confusion. Let's look next at the three secondary combinations: Green, Orange and Violet.

GREEN

Green relates to the fourth energy centre, the **heart** chakra. Fourth out of the traditional seven, it represents the central point of **balance** within a human being, and thus stands as a symbol of **harmony**, just as the Green that occurs in the natural world also stands as a symbol of the harmony of nature. The person who is drawn towards Green is likely to be a **nature lover**, and perhaps herself a natural harmoniser. Green in nature offers fruitfulness and contentment, tranquillity and **hope**. Open fields offer us a feeling of **space**; so do trees, and in looking in all directions at once, they also show us a sense of balance and choice.

Green brings together the qualities of Yellow and of Blue in roughly equal balance. Green is the fulcrum in the middle of the scales, balancing the Blue of divinity with the Yellow of the individual human being. The Green person, in his most harmonious state, demonstrates the fusion and inter-penetration of knowledge and faith, of the personal will of man and a greater, universal Will. He has a balanced appreciation of his unique qualities and gifts, and a sense of **responsibility** about using these to play his part and to make a contribution in the **world**. Being in touch with his heart, he has overcome self-deception. He is aware of his weaknesses but also of his strengths, and is in tune with his personal **truth**. He has a **generous** nature; a heart that is open and **receptive** to those around him; emotions that flow with easy grace and strength. The Green person has a natural sense of **justice** as well as of truth. He enjoys a balanced sense of his own place and purpose, and does not hesitate to take the space he needs, from time to time, for himself. A natural diplomat, with the ability to see all sides of a question, Green also has a sophisticated **social awareness**. Knowing where he is going, too, he is at peace with himself.

Green, in a state of health, is not only in love with the world of nature but also aware of its cycles. Knowing that nothing ever remains the same for very long, she appreciates the **time** available to her and makes an effort to use it well. She also has a well-developed sense of timing, and she may have learned to notice and trust the apparent coincidences that occur in her life; so that she has a way of being in **the right place** at **the right time**. This is indeed a question of trust, and the well-developed Green has come a long way on that journey.

Someone heavily drawn towards the Green energy may, on the other hand, still be searching hard to find some of these qualities. While these attributes are there in potential, at present they are out of reach. In imbalance, the Green person feels himself to be **claustrophobic** and lost in the wood. He does not know when to be where, or where to be when. He may have a great **need for space** and feel unable to ask for it, busying himself always with caring for those around him. He may suffer from frustration in the asserting of his own will, his habit perhaps being to give out constantly to others and then to feel resentment over not finding his own needs met. He may be confused about his own **identity** and bored with the self which seems to be at odds with the world around him. Perhaps he has **deceived** himself in the past about his own weaknesses and is now searching for the truth, in the realisation that he has a responsibility to himself to respect the limitations of time. Instead of a sense of his own true value, he may be **Green with envy**, or even real **jealousy**, of those around him, putting a greater worth on qualities and ways of life which others seem to enjoy than he does on his own. If he can integrate this experience, the jealousy can be turned around and become a strength: the acute observation of others which such jealousy involves can lead him down the path towards an understanding of truth and of humanity itself.

When the Green person overcomes the need for **emotional food** and integrates the full Green quality of the heart, this energy becomes a great gift. An awareness of Green often suggests a **crossroads** in a person's life, offering a new sense of direction and space, and healing the wounds of a broken heart. It may indicate the overcoming of a person's lower needs in favour of a wider vision. Thus the person coming to an appreciation of Green finds a new sense of freedom. The **heart** – healed, open and clear – is the vehicle for the **sharing** of talents and gifts, the giving and receiving of love, the finding of the deepest sense of **integrity** and **truth**.

Pale Green

As with all the paler colours, Pale Green contains both the Green gifts and the challenges in a more intense form. The person coming to this colour may well be at a new and crucial junction. Bored with old habits of self-deception and the wastage of time, she is now searching for the truth on all levels. She has developed a burning sense of **honesty** that will sustain the fullness of reality: its discomforts as well as its solidity. She may have come some way in the journey of transcending the demands of her personal will and acknowledging the supremacy of something wider. Having a balanced sense of **giving** and **receiving**, she is able to be generous without holding back in asking for whatever it is that she sometimes needs for herself. In its most positive form, this ray shows someone who has both discovered her direction and learned the language of the heart.

> *GREEN AFFIRMATION*
> *I have all the space that I need for myself;*
> *within the clarity of this space I live my truth*
> *and follow my path.*

ORANGE

Orange is nothing if not **intense**. The colour relates to the second, or sacral, chakra: an area which has much to do with **emotions**, **instincts**, and **sexuality**. Orange is a colour of the extrovert: this person is **gregarious** and **sociable**. In health and balance, she is poised and self-assured. She enjoys parties and she enjoys action. Whichever gender this person happens to be, he or she is very naturally tuned into body language and the attractions of sex. Usually disinclined to remain for long confined to solitary pursuits, she will seek out the company of other people. She never does things by halves, however; so while she will happily dance the night away, she is also capable of the opposite extreme. The Orange person may, on occasion, be someone with deeply spiritual inclinations. It is just conceivable that this person *might*, like the monks of Tibet, renounce the material world and achieve peace and **bliss** through contemplation and communication, through meditation and prayer, with the world of spirit.

It is a more common pattern, however, for the Orange person to enjoy and require human company. Every party should have at least one Orange guest: his **effervescent, joyful good humour** can raise the spirits of any group and make them laugh, so long as his need for fun does not slip out of control and cause **chaos**. Like the Coral that you will see in the next chapter, however, the Orange often carries a suggestion of **dependency** and **co-dependency** within relationships. It is rare that this person can exist happily as a loner; he may find almost any company to be better than none. The Orange person finds his identity either through his need for the other person, or through his need to be needed. With his inclination to go over the top, he may be in danger of becoming a little **self-indulgent**. This dependent and sometimes indulgent tendency may also lead to **addictions**: to nicotine or whisky, for example, or sex, as well as the more subtle addiction to a partner or a friend. Orange is very much orientated towards **relationship**: in health his relationships are energetic and joyful; when Orange is out of balance, however, his selfishness comes to the fore and he can become wily and **manipulative**.

The selection of Orange often indicates that there has been **shock** or **trauma**, which needs to be addressed before the full picture can emerge. It may suggest a history of some sort of **abuse**, often sexual. On the other hand it can be the very reverse: the person choosing Orange may be someone who enjoys an unusually **happy sexual life**, where this activity brings deep and joyful communication. Orange is a **warm** ray, reminding us of open fires and beautiful sunsets. It relates to the deepest part of the gut, and therefore to **gut feelings** and knowledge. The choice of Orange can indicate that the person is gifted with the capacity for discovering the most profound **insights**. This may be someone of immense vision who has little need for outside teachers, being deeply connected to his or her own inner wisdom. When the problems of shock and dependency are overcome, the choice of Orange indicates **companionship**, **deep understanding** and **bliss**.

ORANGE AFFIRMATION
I flow with the river of my deepest intuition: it is
a sparkling stream that lights my path to joy.

VIOLET

Violet is the colour associated with the **crown**, or the seventh, chakra. It brings together the Red of the earth and the Blue of heaven in equal balance. Reminding us through its fruits of the harvest that another season has come to a close, it is a colour that often signifies **endings** and **new beginnings**. It often indicates **maturity**, or perhaps the completion of a cycle. Like Royal Blue, the consciousness of those drawn to Violet is generally focussed less on the material world and the immediate experience of the senses than upon the more permanent, and more nebulous, world of the **soul** or the **spirit**. This is the philosopher rather than the farmer; the intensive care nurse rather than the laboratory scientist. The person choosing it may well have endured some painful lessons, and silenced the shrill voice of the ego. She has a strong sense of **service** and it is her gifts to others, and frequently the sacrifice of her own needs, that ultimately offer her satisfaction and fulfilment. Being spiritually rather than materially inclined, she tends towards periods of deep **reflection**.

The choice of Violet can signify powerful periods of **change**. It is often these times of disruption that draw a person's attention towards this colour, and that might then encourage him or her to reflect upon the underlying causes for the change. Violet, the colour of transformation, is a reminder to us of the cycle of life and death; it may be helpful to recognise at times what it is in you which needs to die in order to make room for something new.

Violet indicates the possibility of harmony and **equilibrium**. The woman drawn to this hue has an appreciation of her masculine aspect. The man has begun to embrace the woman within himself. From this place of security, both are able to come into relationship with one another. Violet offers the pouring of oil on to troubled waters: it is, of all the rays, the most **calming** and the most deeply **healing**. Those who choose this ray are often those who find themselves involved in the healing of pain or the making of peace.

The Violet person, generally quiet and thoughtful, is given to periods of **despondency** and sometimes **depression**. She may be more of a thinker than a doer, and it can be the weight of her **thinking** that sometimes isolates her and causes her pain. She sometimes, like Blue, feels lonely and left out, perhaps envying those lighter-hearted souls who seem so joyful and free. She needs to avoid the temptation to **control** those with whom she is involved. Her **idealism**, too, contains a caution: it can be the foundation for her greatest achievements, but when it tempts her to deny the reality of her experience it may become a source of suffering. Another trap for Violet is the temptation to slip into feelings of **snobbishness** or some other kind of superiority; if she were to give in to these feelings they would of course lead to a yet deeper experience of loneliness.

Violet can indicate that there has been **grief** and **mourning**. This may be mild, or it may be a profound sadness; even an **escapism** which prevents him from taking responsibility for the practical realities involved in physical life. When this can be overcome, the Violet person may come into the real strength of this ray and connect with the passionate idealism which motivates him to move heaven and earth to bring them both together.

Pale Violet

Where Violet indicates the possibility for transformation, Pale Violet suggests something even deeper and more permanent: the profound change in consciousness which happens when a person has literally metabolised their experience, and which can result in fundamental alterations in a person's way of life. The Pale Violet person, while he has undoubtedly suffered grief and pain and may be extremely vulnerable, nevertheless has the capacity to detach himself from the experience and bring the benefit of it to those around him. He is, in whatever sense this may express itself, a healer; his very presence is soothing. His focussed sense of service gives him a strength that attracts to him many of those who are themselves seeking direction, guidance and wholeness. As he may still be prone, at least from time to time, to bouts of sadness and depression, it sometimes surprises him to find how easily others suppose him to possess a strength that he does not always feel. He has, nevertheless, the ability to support others in a process of difficult change, just as he has sustained such a process in himself.

> ## VIOLET AFFIRMATION
> *The only constant is change: I flow with each new change and trust its power to take me where I need to be.*

chapter 7

TERTIARY COLOURS

Why do you want to open the outside door
when there is an inside door? Everything is within.
Yogaswami
Positive Thoughts for Daily Meditation.

Lastly, there come the tertiary combinations, or combinations of three. Tertiary colours are the most complex mixtures of all, combining the features of the primary and the secondary colours as well as containing their own essence. The colour wheel shows that opposite each tertiary colour appears another colour which is also a tertiary. It also shows that these third combinations appear between each primary and secondary colour. The wheel is one of the most helpful tools for offering you an intuitive grasp of the colours and their relationships. The tertiary colours can be best understood as secondary colours which contain some added primary, leading to an even greater complexity within these hues than within any of the others, since they each contain not only their own quality but also something of the characteristics of both the primary and the secondary colours that flank them. So Turquoise, for example, is a mixture of the Blue and Green which sit on either side of it; but you know that Green is already a marriage of Blue and Yellow. So Turquoise, in addition to being Turquoise and having its own unique character, also contains the influence of the primary colours Blue and Yellow, and of the secondary colour Green. This may sound a little complicated at first, but this impression vanishes once you start using the colours and developing a feel for them. Let's look first at Magenta, which sits in the circle next to Red, and then continue clockwise around the colour wheel.

MAGENTA

Although this colour has a logical place inside the colour circle, it exists outside the traditional rainbow spectrum of colour and the traditional chakra system. This means that it does not have a specific relationship with a particular area of the physical body. This is confirmed in the nature of its energy. Magenta is a **complex** colour, bringing together the **spirituality** of the Violet and the **passion** of the Red; and containing, too, some of the intense **love** quality of the Pink. The person drawn to Magenta may be the Florence Nightingale of her year group. Never one to conform to expectation or the pressure of her peers, she is likely to see beyond the pleasures of the moment. While the others are enjoying the party, she may well be beset by a constant sense of **service**.

This is someone, however, who easily lives inside her head. An **idealist** and often a **pioneer**, her attention is easily engaged by the larger plan; she has little patience with the details. The paperwork is all too easily forgotten, along with the washing up. While this is frequently a difficulty for those linked to the Magenta ray, its converse may be their greatest strength. The person who lives on the positive side of this ray will not only, for example, be a wonderful hostess or teacher, being alert to every person in the room. She is also likely to create beauty in every detail of her surroundings, and even her meals are a work of art. Care and attention are poured into the particularities of all that she addresses, and her home reverberates with love. She is **generous**, **passionate**, **kind**, **tender**, and – sometimes – **impatient**. She gives and works, however, until she drops, and may then become prone to total **despondency**. At times such as these, her family must offer her the same **compassion** she extends to them, for she will quite probably forget that she has ever laughed.

Magenta carries with it a deep sense of commitment to our **purpose** on earth. The Magenta person, while he has probably suffered many hardships and learned many painful lessons, puts a great value on his work and his beliefs. Once he discovers what he believes his purpose to be – and this is quite likely to be something that will serve humanity – he will stop at nothing to achieve it. Once he overcomes his difficulty in being fully in the present, Magenta can develop and finely tune an ability to give a rare degree of **attention**. His **passion is unconditional**; this may on occasion put some strain on those close to him. One of the cautions in the Magenta energy, if he values those close to him, is not to be so **universal** that the personal crumbles around him unnoticed.

Magenta may be a **creative**, radical artist or thinker, way **ahead** of his time. He may hardly notice the likely failure of those around him to acknowledge the value of his work, because the love of the job eclipses for him any other concerns. In health, the Magenta person is deeply **tender**, unconditional in his love, and powerfully committed to everything that he believes in. He is **creative**, **innovative** and **strong**. He has peace of mind and full-flowing physical and emotional energy. His **humility** comes from his acceptance and understanding of the unique value of his own and every other person's contribution to life on earth.

> ## MAGENTA AFFIRMATION
> *Today I notice the details in my surroundings;*
> *I approach every task from a place of love.*

INDIGO

Indigo, or Royal Blue, relates to the **brow** chakra, which connects with that master gland, the pituitary. In health, the person drawn towards this colour is very much his own master: he resembles the conductor whose central place in the orchestra is essential to the rhythm and harmony of the music. Indigo carries **authority** and **stature**: the Indigo person may have a powerful **presence**, inspiring **confidence**, and sometimes fear. Though he may be someone of few words, those that he speaks will probably carry some weight. The Indigo resembles the Blue; but this person is likely to be more **intense**. He is strong, and independent sometimes to the point of **arrogance**. His weaknesses may be those of **haughtiness** and **pride**.

The sense of power the Indigo person often radiates stems, at least in part, from the greater connection she has with those aspects of herself which, for others, remain largely unconscious. This is a quality she is likely to share also with those drawn to Violets. Just as the dark Blue sky of night reveals the stars, so the Indigo person has a vision that penetrates the illusions of the day. She sees with a clarity and **depth** that permeates the maze of the dream-world and understands the way out. She is unlikely, in any situation, to have the wool pulled over her eyes. She is **efficient**, **determined** and very **reliable**. With the Indigo person in the chairman's seat, the management knows that the hoped-for outcome is assured.

Blessed with creativity and penetrating vision, the Indigo person has a powerful **imagination**. Indigo may be the inspired doctor, artist or writer. Or maybe she will be a politician, keeping her cards so naturally, as she does, close to her chest.

The Indigo person has the capacity for clear communication; but his attention may sometimes be focussed on universal rather than personal issues. In imbalance, he may be the **absent-minded** professor who sets the Thames on fire with a new discovery and fails to notice his family's biggest need. He may be **sober** to a fault, living life without a spark of spontaneity or humour. A lover of **mystery** and **surprises**, he may carry this secretive tendency to extremes. And, on occasion, he may suffer the greatest sense of **loneliness**, even **insecurity**, and the deepest **depression** and **despair**. Indigo in imbalance may hold on desperately to whatever is known and familiar, even when this may be something he does not like, in the conviction that the devil he knows is better than the one he does not.

It is rare, however, for Indigo to reach such depths of unhappiness. Her suffering and loneliness are more likely to stem from the awe she inspires in those around her at her rare ability to keep the orchestra playing on even when the ship is appearing to sink. In health, Indigo enjoys her **strength**, her **independence**, and the deep powers of **understanding** with which she is blessed. Her friendship once gained, she is not likely to let you down.

> ## INDIGO AFFIRMATION
> *I am in charge of my feelings and thoughts: I let go of judgment as each day I perceive and understand with deeper vision.*

TURQUOISE

Situated just above but still close to the heart centre, the Turquoise area brings more Blue into the Green energy of the heart. Blue has much to do with communication. The person choosing Turquoise tends to be **expansive** and

creative, with a great desire for deeply **feeling communication**: this is the expression that comes from the heart rather than from the head. Such passionate creativity will lead her towards a way of life which offers her opportunities for **communication on a wide scale**: she may be an artist of some sort; she may write music, poetry or plays; she might make films. She also loves to feel **free**. Artistic pursuits of some sort may work well for her because she does not like to be limited by an imposed structure. Fundamentally **independent**, she may not need the security provided by working for someone else.

The Turquoise person, in good health, has a well-developed sense of **self-responsibility**. He has come some way towards an understanding that he created the situations in which he finds himself. He recognises that freedom and responsibility are two sides of the same coin. His consciousness is likely to be universal: he is the idealist, whose concerns are large and **humanitarian** ones. If he is not a writer or an artist of some sort, he may well be tuned in to current computer and/or media technology, understanding and enjoying the benefits of wide-scale communication in all its aspects.

The choice of Turquoise, just as with all the other colours, may indicate the need for this ray rather than a natural resonance with its qualities. This person may never have found the opportunities he has needed for the full expression of his feelings; so that, rather than having these flow in creative communication, he may feel **distanced** from those around him. Unable to find the peace of heart for which he yearns, he may be finding his **creativity blocked**. He may have long been searching for a sense of direction and still be finding that this eludes him. Turquoise is near to the cool end of the spectrum. Sometimes the choice of Turquoise indicates the tranquillity of the Turquoise sea; perhaps, at another time, this is someone who feels himself to be **alone**, out in the cold. While its choice often suggests someone whose **serenity** allows their creative energy to flow, it may, on the contrary, hint at a sense of **sadness**, or even of the calm before the storm.

The Turquoise person whose energies are flowing loves to **play** and to live **in the moment**. He lives in harmony with his fellow men, allowing them the **freedom** he also enjoys for himself. He allows his emotions to flow, and so he is not afraid to express his **feelings**. He understands the importance of true communication; therefore he can be skilled in listening as in speech. Though he might occasionally fall prey to **delusion** and get carried away on a flight of ideas, his fundamental sense of responsibility will act as a gentle reminder to come down to earth.

Pale Turquoise

This ray differs from Turquoise only in intensity, in the same way as Pale Blue and Pale Yellow relate to their darker siblings. If you are drawn towards this colour, refer to the section on Turquoise and add a few superlatives. You may be extra hard to pin down and control, but you have the capacity to be exceptionally creative in a number of ways, as well as in a wide context, once you decide where to put your energies. And because you have a quite developed sense of responsibility, this is not really so hard for you as it has occasionally felt. You are probably unusual in your **telepathic** nature, which makes you highly aware of the feelings of those around you. Your heart is wide open, so be aware of your need to **protect** it sometimes.

> *TURQUOISE AFFIRMATION*
> *My emotions flow freely; I am strong and*
> *creative in the expression of all that I understand*
> *through my heart.*

OLIVE GREEN

It is the colour Olive Green which has covered the surface of the physical world – presumably – since time began. Lichen and moss, grass and the **new leaves** in Spring, all tend towards a shade of Green whose essence is distinct from the more popular Greens which have traditionally formed a part of people's clothes and furnishings. This essence has its origin, and perhaps its power, in the combination of Yellow and Green which together form the colour Olive. When Green inclines towards Yellow, we feel the youthfulness and the vernal force of nature. It is the Olive Green of spring mornings that brings **hope** and **joy** for the fruits of summer. This is the colour of chlorophyll and the vitality of nature offered through the plant: Olive thus has the power to **heal** and **regenerate** on many levels. It is a colour of great strength: it often repels before it later attracts us quite powerfully.

Those drawn to the colour Olive are often individuals who have experienced considerable pain, and who have had to work to regain the power to direct and control their lives. These are people of **stamina** and **determination**. They have, like olive trees, felt the need to dig deep in stony ground to find for themselves the sustenance which their outer world has failed to provide. They have, like those in Noah's Ark, survived all sorts of tests. The olive branch is the **peace offering** and the **promise of reward**. It is the wisdom born of experience and shared with the world. A challenge within this ray is to avoid the trap of mis-using the **power** that Olive can bestow. Olive is a **bridge**. We share with the rest of the animal kingdom the concerns of the lower energy centres: those of survival; in other words food, warmth, shelter, and reproduction. These also present other issues, such as dependency and co-dependency, competition for resources and for personal power. The challenge for humankind is to raise our consciousness beyond these issues and expand the gift of our humanity. It is Olive that offers a bridge between these lower concerns and the area of the heart; and it is through the **heart** that we can bring our understanding into a shared space, overcoming the voice of the ego in response to the wider world.

The choice of Olive may indicate that a person is harbouring **bitterness**, also within the heart, and needs the powerful balm of this colour to help him to release this emotion. It may show that, like some of those military people whose working life puts them daily into Olive, he is **rigid** and **unbending**, finding it difficult to go with the flow of experience. In its happy state, however, Olive shows a healthy balance between **feeling and thought**; between the individual self and the wider world. It brings the happiness and joy of the Yellow energy into the emotional body. It is a colour of **leadership** in the most positive sense: the connection of man or woman with the depths of their feminine, creative aspect, bringing **clarity** and **direction** into the mind and the heart.

> ## OLIVE GREEN AFFIRMATION
> *I overcome every hurdle with joyful persistence,*
> *knowing that each step brings me nearer to the*
> *doorway of my own heart and my own truth.*

GOLD

This colour brings together the warmth and the instinctive quality of Orange and the sharp sunshine clarity of Yellow. Gold is all **warmth** and **humour**, **wisdom** and **joy**. Those habitually drawn to this colour tend to display characteristics of **strength** and **courage**, and **natural leadership**. This is a colour of **royalty**. It carries with it a sense of **value** and worth. The "Gold" person finds his natural position at the centre of any group. He is **generous**, finding great pleasure in giving to those around him and so creating a sense of fertile abundance in his activities and his relationships.

Those choosing Gold may, on the one hand, have already developed a sense of their individual value, or they may be searching for it. The person who is well tuned to the Gold energy, like the Orange, has a connection with her own **inner wisdom**. Rather than turn to an outside authority, she knows that the answers to most questions can be found within herself. Where the Orange, however, is all instinct and guts, Gold has more of a connection with the **intellect**. She has the capacity for deep **insights** and understanding based not only on intuition but also on a strong reasoning power. She has a **powerful**, **projective** type of energy, and a natural tendency to **protect** those around her: it is hardly surprising that others turn easily to her for guidance and support.

On the other hand, the choice of Gold may sometimes indicate deep and **irrational fear** which cannot be argued away by force of reason. The Gold person may be one who has suffered great difficulty in assimilating painful experiences; he may be, therefore, **acutely anxious** and **nervous**. He may be terrified of the dark, frightened of flying, obsessed with the locking of doors. Rather than feeling clear and self-confident, the person choosing Gold may suffer **grave self-doubt** and **confusion**. The need here is to embrace the fear and confusion and discover what it has to teach. Gold then carries with it the promise of a wonderful **clarity** and **conviction**.

The Gold person in a healthy state radiates a quality of **warmth** and **joy**, and is often great **fun** to be with. He has a ready sense of humour. He is good company and very **stimulating**. His mind is always active: a field fertile with new **ideas**. Like the scientist or the philosopher, he is always willing to experiment and, if necessary, to change his mind. He is both the **teacher** and the **student**: never bored, he is not only open to new discovery and knowledge, but also gently aware, quite often, of his own and others' absurdity.

Gold's natural quality of royalty may get the better of him from time to time. His Gold energy can become unbalanced, as can all our other energies. Beware, on such occasions, the tendency in him to value his own opinion far above those of his friends and associates. He can be a fearful **egotist**. In this tipsy state, the love of this colour might also indicate not only **greed**, **egotism** or **false humility**, but instead another type of imbalance: genuine and painful **self-doubt**. This might make him vulnerable to **glamour**, when he may forget that all that glitters is not Gold. The Gold person can, Shylock-like, deceive not only himself but those around him, occasionally taking the path of the **coward**. Gold has a natural power: the caution, and the great gift, is to use it well.

In its naturally happy and harmonious state, the Gold is a wonderful and joyous energy, demonstrating the **generosity** and **benevolence** of a strong leader, the **wisdom** of Solomon, the **discrimination** of a sage and the **kindness** of a good parent.

GOLD AFFIRMATION
It is inside myself that I hold the answers to all my questions, and the key to my destiny.

CORAL

Coral combines the energies of Red and Pink and Orange, with even a touch of what is contained within Gold. Coral contains the energy of unconditional love associated with Pink, and combines this with qualities of wisdom and under-standing. Being at the hotter end of the spectrum, Coral is a **warm** colour. The person drawn to Coral has a strong sense of **family** and **community** and feels the need to be part of a closely-knit group. Always sensitive to the needs of those around him, he has a deeply **empathetic** quality. When Coral's friend is in trouble, he will climb right into that person's shoes. He tends, however, to keep his own feelings hidden for fear of being wounded. He is, in fact, highly **vulnerable**, like the coral organism itself which hides inside a **shell** of protection.

Like Pink, Coral carries a tendency towards over-generosity. Coral often suffers from a lack of the belief in her own value and will thus, quite easily, fall prey to situations of **unrequited love**. She is quite likely to fall in love with someone way beyond her reach: her teacher, her doctor, or perhaps the husband of someone else. More often than not, she is well aware that this person has probably not even noticed her. The choice of Coral may indicate that there has been some kind of **abuse** in the past and that the person needs to discover a belief in her own individuality and self-worth. In a Coral state, a person may feel **over-dependent** upon those around her, unable to believe in her ability to fend for herself. Such dependency often manifests as some kind of **addictive** behaviour: the dependency, for example, on alcohol, drugs, nicotine, comfort food or another person. The other side of this coin is the capacity within Coral for forming deep and **loyal** personal friendships; and the Coral person will tend not only to feel part of, but also to have a sense of responsibility for, the wider community. She has a deep instinctive knowledge that everything is interconnected.

Coral's **emotions** run deep. This is a person who acts not so much on what she thinks as on what she feels. Yet many of these feelings are so deep that they can be very hard to access and understand. Just as the coral organism grows deep within the sea, so the feelings and motivations of the Coral person lie deeply buried within the unconscious. Once she gains an understanding of these hidden forces within her, Coral can gain access to a depth of **wisdom** and **insight** which gives extra force to her qualities of **empathy** and **imagination**.

The Coral person has a sense of **continuity through time** and an ability to see and understand, both for herself and others, the lessons of the past, so that the wisdom of these may be brought into the present situation. This person puts a great value on the quality of family life and she is highly **sensitive to beauty**. She is therefore likely to be warm and creative within the home. The Coral quality, in health, renders this person an invaluable companion, having an abundance of **kindness**, **wisdom** and **warmth**.

CORAL AFFIRMATION
It is through my vulnerability that I find true communion with those I love. I have the courage to be vulnerable.

There is one final "colour" which is found to be very helpful in colour therapy, even though it is not, in fact, a colour in the same way as the hues just described: this is White. White is actually the resolution of all the other hues, the pure full-spectrum light before it becomes prismatically divided into the rainbow hues and tints.

WHITE

White is the **blank page** of all colour. It is everything and it is nothing. This person, like quicksilver, may be everywhere and nowhere; it might be hard to pin her down. The choice of White may indicate in the person choosing it a quiet, confident feeling of **balance**, **depth** and **breadth**. It might, on the other hand, betray a sense of **emptiness**. This might be someone who has **innocence** and **purity**; and who is, perhaps, also a little **naïve**; or she might be someone who is unwilling to confront her own **shadow**, ignoring whatever it is that she does not want to face.

White is sometimes **transparently** clear, sometimes **invisible**. Now you see her, now you don't. What you do see however, in a close relationship with White, is yourself. White is a **mirror** and a shining **light**; she has the potential to perceive with **crystal clarity** in those around her what is not always apparent to others. This somehow becomes clear to her friends even without any conscious intention on the part of White to reflect home truths. This can cause the White person discomfort and pain in close encounters; but her friendships, once secured, have a richness and a depth which will thoroughly reward the moments of unease.

White is a colour of great **intensity**. In Christianity and the West, it is associated with rituals of **purity**: baptism, first communion, confirmation and marriage; in China, it is associated with funerals and the escorting of the departed into the purity of heaven. The person choosing White may have endured **fierce suffering**; he has also lived and learned intensely. In choosing White, he may indicate that at present he feels **washed out**, by **grief** or sheer **exhaustion**. There may have been a time of **clearing** and **cleansing**, incorporating the experiences of the past as he prepares for a new phase of his life. He has chosen the path of all or nothing. Given to extremes, he knows the rising waves of joy as well as the deepest pits of sorrow.

He is quite probably someone of **broad intellect**, having the capacity to apply his mind without undue effort to mathematics or philosophy, the movement of the stock market or the history of Hindu thought. This may, indeed, be someone who has suffered from too much choice; so that it has been hard for him to find what it is that will engage his commitment. He may already have pursued a number of different goals. He is, too, a **perfectionist**; so that he makes things difficult for himself; though the results he eventually achieves may well reward him for this trait. He has the potential for a rare degree of roundedness; once his true direction is perceived, he is likely to find the strands of his experience weaving themselves, eventually, to form a rich, deep tapestry.

WHITE AFFIRMATION
I understand and release the mistakes of the past; I see each new day with greater clarity than before.

• • • • •

So much for some of the properties of the individual colours. These are guidelines: for those who wish to study colour symbolism in greater depth, there is more information available (see Further Reading). On pages 89–92 you will find a Table, which summarises the salient features associated with each colour; it also includes some suggestions for sources of these rays in foods and crystals, flowers and aromatic essences. In this instance, for the sake of simplicity, the colours are listed in the order in which they appear in the spectrum. The colours are also approached in a different way in a series of guided colour journeys, or visual-isations which are given in the Appendix at the back of this book, and which are also available separately, on a compact disc: this makes the colour vibration of these visualisations very easily accessible.

Each of these colours is, of course, part of the whole spectrum. Like brothers and sisters, there is an inescapable connection between them. Like brothers and sisters, too, there are aspects in which they support one another and others in which they may, from time to time, clash. Human beings are not amoeba-like single cells. We are multi-levelled beings of massive complexity. We have shades of all colours and we change through time. We do, however, relate very closely to one or two colours more than others. For some, this comes as an instant recognition; for others, the process of recognising their "true" colours may take longer. What our true colour (or colours) is becomes increasingly clear as we open ourselves to working with colour in numerous ways.

Some schools of colour therapy also include other hues, such as — among others — cream and brown and black and grey and silver. These are not included here for a number of reasons, including the fact that they do not occupy a clear place in the traditional spectrum. Black, for instance, is technically the absence of colour, being the absorption of all light rather than the selective reflection of some of its vibrations. Brown comes, as all artists know, with the random mixing of other colours. For those particularly drawn to any of these colours, there is a certain amount of information available in other books.

COLOUR	QUALITIES	DIFFICULTIES	BODY AREA	FOODS	CRYSTALS/GEMS	ESSENTIAL OILS	FLOWERS
Red	Courage	Over-concern with	Hands	Red peppers	Ruby	Myrrh	Carnation
	Determination	material/survival	Feet	Beetroot	Garnet	Patchouli	Dahlia
	Extrovert	Anger	Legs	Radishes		Vetivert	Freesia
	Grounded	Resentment	Pubic area	Red meat			Tulip
		Violence		Strawberries			Paeony
				Currants			Red hot poker
				Cherries			
Pink	Unconditional love	Emptiness	Reproduction	Watermelon	Rose quartz	Rose	Rose
	Compassion	Need to be liked/		Salmon	Pink tourmaline		Hollyhock
	Intuition	loved			Rhodocrozite		Carnation
	Tenderness	Childishness					Dahlia
	Generosity	Sentimentality					Tulip
	Forgiveness						
Coral	Love with wisdom	Dependency	Lower abdomen	Mango	Coral	Apricot Brandy
	Loyalty	Co-dependency		Squash	Peach aventurine		Begonia
	Empathy	Unrequited love		Peaches			Azalea
	Love of beauty			Apricots			
				Melons			
Orange	Vitality	Dependency	Mid–Lower	Carrots	Carnelian	Ginger	Tiger flower
	Sociability	Co-dependency	Abdomen	Pumpkins	Orange topaz	Sandalwood	Oriental poppy
	Sexuality	Shock		Orange peppers		Neroli	Lily
	Self-assurance	Trauma		Egg yolks		Tangerine	
	Gut instincts	Self-indulgence		Oranges			
	Bliss	Addiction		Satsumas			

COLOUR	QUALITIES	DIFFICULTIES	BODY AREA	FOODS	CRYSTALS/GEMS	ESSENTIAL OILS	FLOWERS
Gold	Wisdom	Confusion	Solar plexus/	Swedes	Gold topaz	Sandalwood	Marigold
	Joy	Self-doubt	Mid-abdomen	Pineapple	Amber	Lemon	Montbretia
	Insight	Irrational fear	Nervous system	Melons	Gold		Sunflower
	Gut knowledge	Phobias	Spine				
	Humour	Deception					
	Discrimination						
Yellow	Rational intelligence	Nervous anxiety	Solar plexus	Butter	Citrine	Lemon	Sunflower
	Clear thinking	Confusion fear	Nervous system	Sweetcorn	Calcite	Citronella	Daffodil
	Happiness	Greed/power/ego	Skin	Yellow peppers	Tiger's eye		Primrose
	Individuality	Difficulties with		Grapefruit			Evening primrose
	Personal power	assimilation (mental/		Lemons			St John's Wort
	Optimism	emotional/physical)					
Pale Yellow	Decisiveness	Extreme fear	Solar plexus	Butter	Citrine	Lemon	Daffodil
	Deep self-knowledge	Extreme confusion	Nervous system	Sweetcorn	Calcite	Citronella	Crocus
	Clear logical thought		Skin	Yellow peppers			Freesia
				Grapefruit			
				Lemons			
Olive Green	Leadership	Rigidity	Solar plexus/Heart	Fresh green salad	Jade	Pine	
	Stamina	Bitterness		Green olives	Moldavite		
	Persistence	Abuse of power					
	Strength						

COLOUR	QUALITIES	DIFFICULTIES	BODY AREA	FOODS	CRYSTALS/GEMS	ESSENTIAL OILS	FLOWERS
Green	Truth Jealousy Justice Openness Balance Integrity Co-operation Direction	Prejudice Envy Over-generosity Loss of direction	Heart Lungs Chest	All green vegetables	Emerald Malachite Green tourmaline	Bergamot Melissa	
Pale Green	Seeker of truth Honesty Humility	Lost their way	Heart Lungs	Fresh green salad	Fluorite	Bergamot Melissa	
Turquoise	Creative expression Freedom Responsibility Playfulness	Loneliness Coolness Feelings of rejection	Upper chest Immune system	Asparagus	Turquoise Aquamarine Fluorite		
Blue	Peacefulness Serenity Clear communication Independence	'Father issues' Problems with authority Loneliness	Throat	Blueberries Black grapes	Sapphire Sodalite Laramar	Camomile Lavender	Forget-me-not Bluebell Campanula
Pale Blue	Faith Trust	Intense loneliness Difficult communication	Throat		Sapphire Laramar	Camomile	

COLOUR	QUALITIES	DIFFICULTIES	BODY AREA	FOODS	CRYSTALS/GEMS	ESSENTIAL OILS	FLOWERS
Indigo	Imagination	Arrogance	Brow area	Black grapes	Lapis lazuli	Frankincense	Iris
	Clairvoyance	Intolerance		Blackberries	Sodalite		Anemone
	Integration of abilities	Depression					
		Isolation					
Violet	Idealism	Melancholy	Crown	Purple broccoli	Amethyst	Lavender	Lavender
	Dedication	Depression		Red cabbage	Tanzanite	Frankincense	Lilac
	Transformation	Grief/mourning		Aubergines			Cyclamen
	Self-sacrifice	Superiority					Crocus
	Service	Fanaticism					African violet
	Spirituality	Pessimism					
	Healing	Alienation					
Pale Violet	Transmutation of	Intense sadness	Crown		Pale amethyst	Lavender	Lilac
	negative experience	Bereavement			Fluorite		
	to positive	Grief					
Magenta	Highest order of love	Melancholy	Above crown	Plums	Lapidalite		Cineraria
	Sense of quality	Desire					Azalea
	Attention to detail	Unreality					Rhododendron
White	Clarity	Emptiness	Whole body	Milk	Clear quartz	Jasmine	Snowdrop
	Understanding	Intense suffering		Potatoes	Diamond		Carnation
	Equilibrium	Perfectionism					Rose
							Jasmine

chapter 8

LIKE ATTRACTS LIKE: OPPOSITES ATTRACT?

Without contraries is no progression. Attraction and repulsion,
reason and energy, love and hate, are necessary to human existence.

William Blake

The Marriage of Heaven and Hell

Sometimes you may hear that "like attracts like"; then, perhaps, you are told that "opposites attract". Both statements are true. Whether you are attracted to another person because of their comforting sense of similarity to yourself, or because of the qualities in them that contrast with your own, there is usually, as was suggested in Part One, a hidden agenda that is not apparent at first. It is helpful to look at some of the different aspects of colour which may show you where you and your close friends come in the spectrum, and the ways in which you might be likely to interact. Because, just as there is "chemistry" between people, so there are also relationships between the colours that people choose. Colours, like people, come from all parts of the spectrum. It can be said quite accurately that they have different "vibes". Like the many facets of a diamond, each colour represents an aspect of the whole. But, like the members of any other family, they have different personalities and relate to one another in varying ways. So, when you want to get a handle on what is going on between you and another person, you need to take a look at the way in which the colours you choose relate to theirs.

How well might a "Red" person get along with a "Turquoise" one? In what ways might a "Green" person harmonise with a "Violet" one, and in what ways might they find themselves sometimes out of sympathy? Might Magenta and bright Yellow like each other, or are they more likely to clash? What might your choice of Coral have to show you about the way you interact with a partner who is more drawn towards Indigo? In order to answer any of these questions, it is necessary to investigate some of the inter-relationships between the colours themselves, as an understanding of these connections can offer surprising and enjoyable insights into the dynamics of your personal interactions. Suppose you are strongly drawn to Indigo as your first choice, while someone close to you has come down in favour of Coral: there are several things to bear in mind when it comes to comparing your colours. At this point, we are considering mainly your first choice of colour, which yields a lot of helpful information about your fundamental tendencies and qualities; later on, we will look more specifically at the significance of the subsequent selections that you make.

The Spectrum

First of all, there is the spectrum. From which end of the spectrum do your choices come? The Red end is the hottest and the most stimulating; it is also, which sometimes sounds like a contradiction in terms, the slower end. What you perceive as the colour Red is light vibrating on a longer and slower wavelength than the light at the other end, which vibrates faster. The Violet end is the coolest and the most soothing; it is also the fastest. This already offers you a few clues about the predispositions of people drawn towards various colours. A phrase such as "hot-blooded", for example, immediately conjures up a picture of Red rather than Pale Violet; whereas the Blue robes of a Madonna create a picture of serenity. So the Indigo person suggested above, being temperamentally near to the cooler end of the spectrum, is likely to be calm and placid – altogether "cool", possibly in all senses of that word; while his Coral friend, near to the fiery end, is probably more emotional and more obviously demonstrative. Indigo is also predominantly a Blue colour. This indicates that the basic constitutional tendencies of this person are likely to be nearer to the Blue acquisitive and introspective ones than to the Red extrovert and reactionary ones, or the Yellow joyful if slightly nervy ones. Coral, on the other hand, is closer to Red than to Yellow, and contains no Blue at all: we can take it that this person's dominant tendencies relate to the Red energy; though there is a hidden suggestion of some Yellow qualities as well.

Chakras as Pointers

The next helpful tool for your interpretation kit is the association of the colours with the different chakras, or energy stations, up and down the body (Fig. 1, p. 97). The Red end of the spectrum is closest to earth, relating to the hands, feet and legs; while the Violet end is closest to the sky, or heaven, and relates to the head. Again, this offers you a number of hints. Indigo, right next to Violet, relates to the upper part of the body, and specifically to the head; Coral, on the other hand, corresponds to the gut. So while this Indigo person may have a tendency to live in his thoughts, and to space out in a "heavenly", or at any rate abstract, world of ideas and ideals, his Coral companion is more likely to be pretty thoroughly anchored in the immediate world, and she perhaps relies on her gut instincts more than on the logic of her rational mind. She, of course, has her own difficulties; and among these may be the tendency to find herself to be both more earth-bound and also less rational than she would like (or, and this is sometimes more to the point, more than *he*, her Indigo friend, would like). With his rapid rate of vibration, Indigo may process ideas and thoughts with the speed of lightning, while Coral may take a little longer.

Are you hot or cool, or somewhere in the middle? Do you incline more towards the physical or the mental; do you prefer to spend your time in the gym or with your head in a good book; or do you feel the need to strike a balance? Are you an ideas person, with your head in the clouds; do you have two feet firmly on the ground; or are you happily poised between the two? Do you process ideas easily and quickly (the Violet end of the spectrum); or do you prefer to take time to test things out in a practical way to discover whether they work (the Red end of the spectrum)? Are you basically a **"Blue"** person; do you hold on to all your familiar possessions, and enjoy the security offered by solid structures and a good sense of discipline? Are you a **"Red"** person, charging out to meet the world in a stream of dynamic activity? Are you a **"Yellow"** person, with a dedication to making sure that life is fun for all concerned, "feeling the fear and doing it anyway" (or not)?

The apparent trivia of the daily domestic scene are often of far greater significance in the quality of most people's relationships than larger questions such as our belief systems. If you are someone who has a great need for tidiness, for example, and you live with someone who leaves cupboard doors open and decorates the carpets with dirty socks, it may soon be small consolation that your musical tastes and the subjects in which you majored are very similar......The first step in the communication which is essential to avoid the slippery slope towards the point of no return is to understand what makes both you and the other person tick: whether, for example, your need is a reasonable one rather than obsessive, or why it is that the other person finds it so difficult to function in an organised way.

The first rule for successful negotiation is to understand where the other person is coming from. Are the untidy habits coming from a **Red** tendency to achieve a lot and to be – as a by-product of this – impulsive, impatient, always on to the next thing before the first one is finished? Or are they coming from a **Violet** inclination to be off in space somewhere instead of getting on with the job in hand? And is your need for tidiness coming from your **Green** sense of the harmony and order necessary and inherent in a beautiful world, or is it because you are a **Yellow** and **Gold** control freak; or someone who concentrates – in perhaps a **Red** way – on the practical things in order to avoid the wider issues?

> *The first rule for successful negotiation is to understand where the other person is coming from.*

In addition to the understanding which the spectrum, together with the language of colour, offers you, the colour wheel also gives insights into the specific ways in which colours complement and juxtapose one another. It shows not only the gradations of colour that we saw in Chapters 5, 6 and 7 – from the simple and straightforward primaries through to the complexity of their mixtures – but also the juxtaposition of various colours with one another. It shows how, yes, like does attract like at exactly the same time as opposites attract.

The combination of several aspects of colour insights have already given you, as it were, a new pair of spectacles to peer through the looking glass of colour and discover some explanations about yourself and your loved ones that have perhaps eluded you in the past. Complementary colours are very useful in understanding the application of colour in inter-personal dynamics. The significant point is that every pair of complementary colours between them **contains all the three primaries**; and all of the three primary colours together contain the full spectrum of light. This means, when you apply this principle to people, that two people choosing complementary opposite colours to one another have the potential to complete and fulfil one another in all

Chakra

7. Crown

6. Brow

5. Throat

4. Heart

3. Solar Plexus

2. Sacral

1. Base

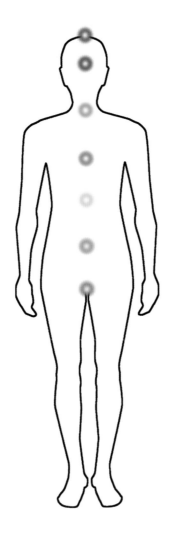

FIGURE 1: The Seven Major Chakras

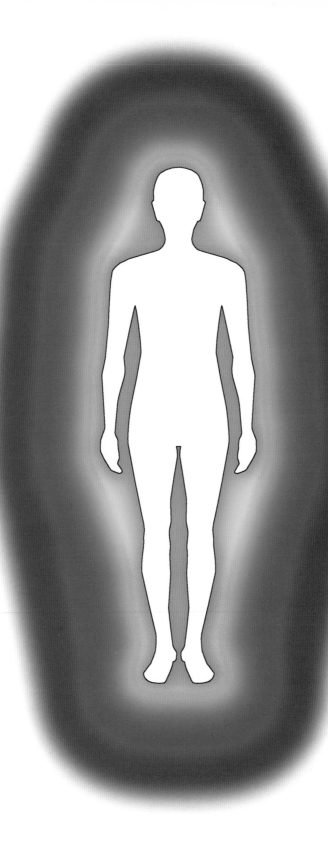

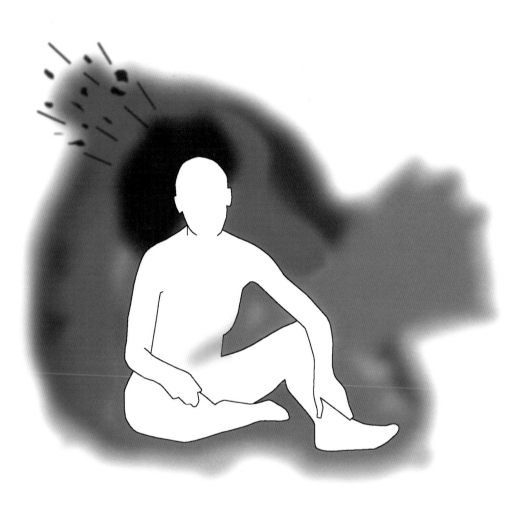

FIGURE 2, LEFT: An Idealised Image of the Human Aura in Perfect Balance

FIGURE 3, ABOVE: The Aura of an Individual in Imbalance: (the area around the head indicates mental illness; the darkness suggests depression; the leaking of Orange points to major trauma)

These colours are also shown on
the perforated inner sections of
the book cover, as cut-out cards.

magenta

pale violet

violet

indigo

pale blue

blue

pale turquoise

turquoise

FIGURE 4: Twenty Spectral Hues and Tints

Which are your
favourite colours?

red
pink
pale pink
coral
orange
gold
yellow
pale yellow
olive green
green

Choose your colour
preferences from your cards,
then check any card against
this chart to identify its
name correctly.

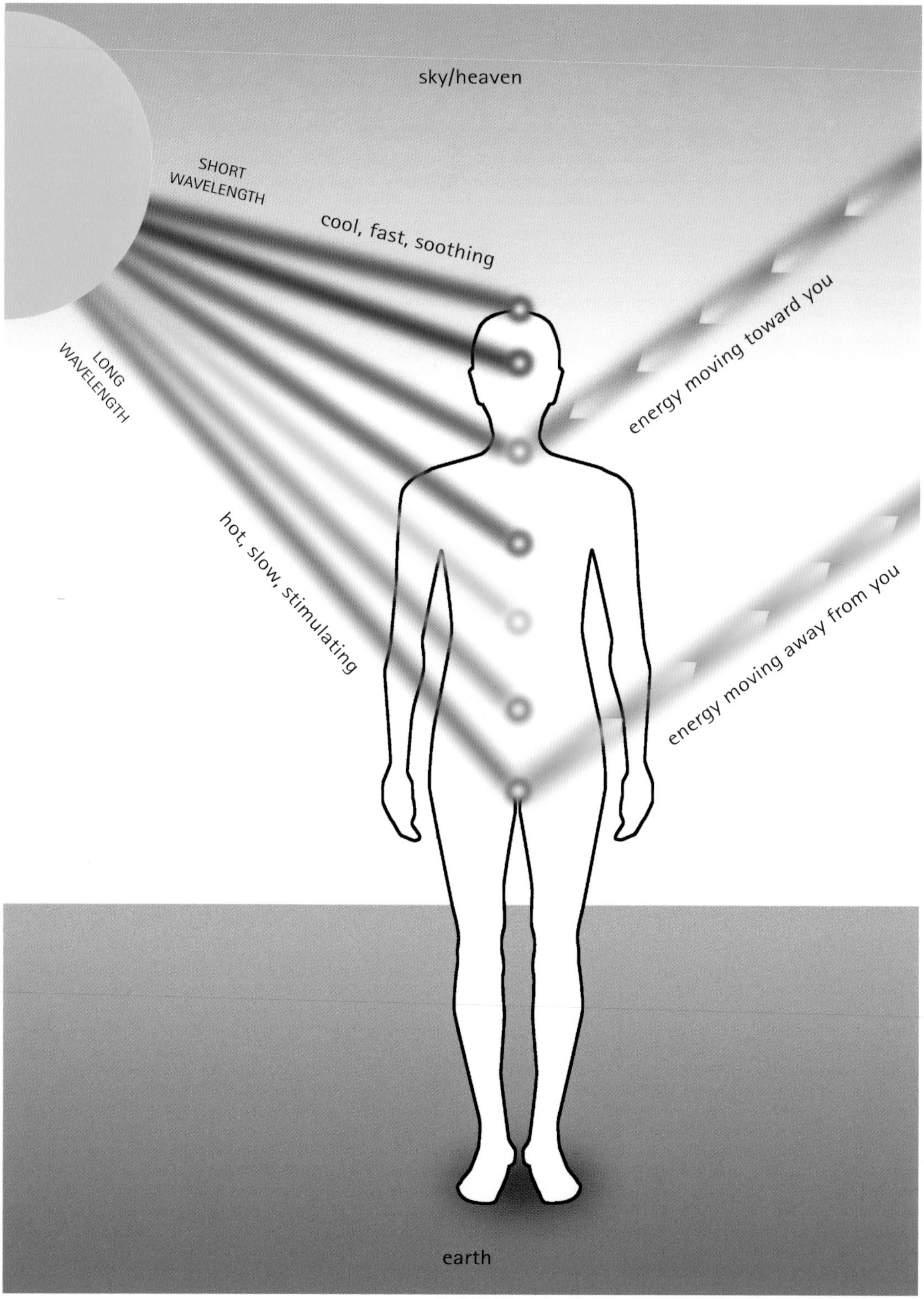

sky/heaven
SHORT WAVELENGTH
cool, fast, soothing
LONG WAVELENGTH
hot, slow, stimulating
energy moving toward you
energy moving away from you
earth

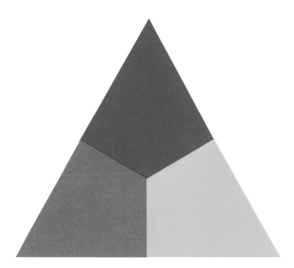

FIGURE 6: The Primary Colours

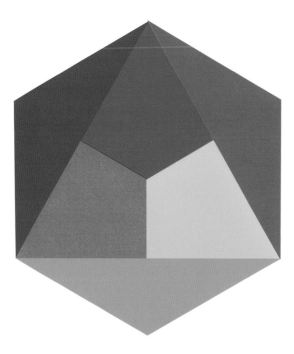

FIGURE 7: The Primary and Secondary Colours

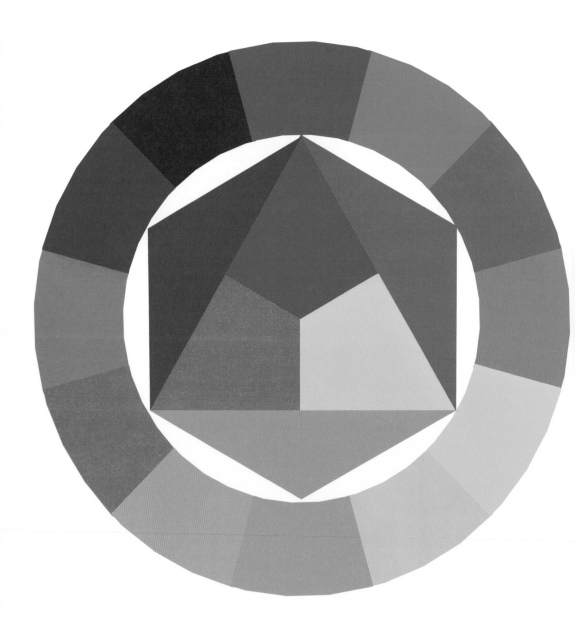

FIGURE 8: The Colour Wheel, or Circle, showing Primary, Secondary and Tertiary Colours

sorts of ways! Because, while these colours are opposite to one another, they are also complementary: in other words, the energies of one can balance and complete the energies of the other. The theory behind this has to do with the principle of colour harmony. Harmony in this sense has nothing to do with your subjective preferences: rather than combinations of colours – let's say, different shades of Blue and Turquoise, for example – which blend together without sharp contrasts, it implies something much more radical. It implies a law of balance and the symmetry of forces. It has to do, in fact, with the **law of polarity** that we looked at in the first section. Through colour, you can find the means to balance and complete one another, instead of remaining out of touch with one another at one end of whatever spectrum relates to the issue in hand. These colours, at one and the same time, are both the exact opposite of one another and also, being interdependent, they can be both profoundly sympathetic towards and supportive of one another.

Let us imagine some close pairs of friends. Each of the pair is being given a gender, simply for illustration. **Please note** that this is entirely arbitrary and does not imply that any colour is weighted towards either end of the physical gender spectrum. As before, we shall work clockwise around the colour circle, beginning with the colour Red, whose complementary colour is Green.

RED AND GREEN

Her predominant choice is Red; his is Green. Her energy – **passionate** and **determined** – could, in this case, be described as rather more masculine than his, which is of an open, receptive, feminine nature. She is an **innovator**. Full of **fire** and **enthusiasm**, she tends to drive and motivate not only herself but also those around her. He loves her **vitality**, but sometimes he needs to make a gentle retreat and find a space to slow the breath. These two are not so much co-dependent as inter-dependent. He is the heart; she is the rush of blood. She is the redness of earth; he is the Green leaves that spring from it. Red is highly motivated and full of plans; Green provides the **space**, as well as a degree of **balance**, in which these plans can find expression. When Red goes over the top, Green can restore her **equilibrium**. When Red gets mad, Green is the most likely one to make her see reason; though at times he may need to move away from the heat.

Green is **open-hearted**, **loving** and **generous**. Sometimes, he may be a bit too passive, especially in regard to asking for what he needs for himself. Red's active **dynamism** could therefore overwhelm him from time to time; but in good balance, she will help him to learn to assert his needs. Red has her feet firmly on the ground; and while she appreciates Green's **kindness** and **generosity** to those around him, she will ensure that their survival needs are not jeopardised by it. Red is, on the whole, the more **practical** of the two; while Green takes a **panoramic view** of their lives as well as of the wider world, Red is clearly focussed on the job in hand. This, however, can sometimes mean that her feet get well and truly stuck in the mud, and she is grateful in retrospect that Green had the wisdom to **broaden** her horizons a little and raise her vision. Red, with all her determination and power, can also be very **stubborn**; it is Green's **breadth** and **imagination** which he can skilfully harness here to show her, through gentle persuasion, another way.

Green, whose tendency to open his heart too wide can leave him feeling a little empty, may suffer by envying others, or even feeling **jealous**. Red, so long as she has resisted the temptation to tread all over him like a garden footpath, can help him by showing him how to protect his own needs and space. When he loses his sense of **direction**, Red – her two feet on the ground – can help him find it. The powerful **commitment** which Red is happy to make in loving Green may help him to put a greater value on himself and what he has to offer, so that he has no more need to envy others. Red, always practical and down-to-earth, is also a **realist**. Green, who has a fundamental love of the **truth**, can at times lose his balance: just as, in his generosity, he may lay himself open to deceit from others, so, in his zealous search for personal growth, he may occasionally give in to **self-deception**. Red, always one to call a spade a spade, is likely to confront him head-on until he sees his mistake.

Red is not good at waiting. If she wants to do something, she wants to do it **now**. That is how she gets her fingers burned. Green, in this respect, is her teacher. Green has a natural sense of space and time and **rhythm**: he moves naturally in harmony with the cycles of nature. If Red is thwarted in her plans, she will either give in to feelings of **resentment** and **frustration**, or forget the plan and find one that provides quicker rewards. Green, with his eternal sense of **trust** and **hope**, may see the wisdom in the original plan and know that it pays to wait.

Red's way of loving is passionate and often generous; but it may be **conditional**. It may depend for its sustenance on **gratification**, and perhaps on a little recognition.

Green, on the other hand, is a natural **harmoniser**; he does not mind working behind the scenes. Where Red's reward may sometimes be personal gratification, Green – orientated towards the **community** – is satisfied by the knowledge that a job is well done. In an extreme case, however, there are few whose beliefs surpass the passionate commitment of the Red; she will, if necessary, make the ultimate **sacrifice** for those around her. If he is wise, Green knows this, and the knowledge sustains him during those times when Red is driving her steam roller.

Red, in almost any situation, may **react** quite strongly to people and circumstance; Green can help her to stand back. Green, always willing and able to see every side of an argument, may find it very difficult, at times, to come to a firm opinion or decision. It is on these occasions that he will happily overlook Red's tendency towards wild prejudice in the grateful acknowledgment that she can always be relied upon, if called to do so, to make up his mind for him!

Red is the generator and the driving force; Green is the gentle discipline that balances the passion and gives it direction and purpose. Together, they balance the elements of their joint nature; when communication is good, they can co-exist in passion, loyalty and mutual trust.

MAGENTA AND OLIVE GREEN

If she chooses Olive Green and he is drawn towards Magenta (or, indeed, the other way around), we have another interesting pair. Olive is a lover of nature, perhaps of animals, and certainly of wide open spaces. Olive loves to feel the soles of her feet in firm touch with the fresh grass. Magenta, too, may love all this in theory; it is quite likely, however, that the new leaves will unfold without his noticing them because his mind is engaged on a large project or idea. Magenta is an **idealist**; he is probably quite **passionate** about causes. He may champion the local Save the Trees campaign; but it is up to Olive to persuade him to do an hour's gardening if she is not to finish up doing it all herself. Magenta is quite capable of spending whole days absorbed in a task of writing about the beauty of nature, perhaps forgetting even to open the curtains; Olive, meanwhile, is busy in the sunshine, either digging the weeds or painting the flowers.

Magenta is a natural **healer**. His hands, his voice, his gentle manner all act as vehicles for the energy which moves through him often unnoticed. This is someone whose simplest touch seems to relieve pain and anxiety. This can be of great comfort to Olive, who may have suffered a great deal of pain in her life. Olive is someone of **stamina** and **determination**; she may have grown accustomed to hardship and had to soldier on alone, finding her own sustenance from within. Magenta is her soothing balm. They understand each other well. Olive and Magenta may both, however, recognise from time to time a similarity in those aspects of themselves which have caused them pain: while Magenta may be harbouring hidden anger, Olive, too, may hold on to **bitterness** from the past. And while Magenta has the capacity to help Olive to let go of this bitterness, life has quite probably not been an easy ride for him, either. Someone of deep feelings, he has often been burdened with pain, both his own and others'. It is often the trials he has experienced which have given Magenta the **strength** and the **understanding** to support those who turn to him in difficult circumstances.

Olive is a natural, if quiet, leader. Her strength comes from the heart. A person of natural integrity and truth, Olive inspires confidence and **trust** in those around her. In fact, it may well be a similarity in the quality of Olive and Magenta which originally brought about their mutual recognition. Like Magenta, the energy of Olive is **strengthening** and **restorative**. Where Magenta's healing quality stems from a spiritual strength and transcendent sense of purpose, Olive's may show itself in ways which are physical and practical. Like the new leaves in spring, Olive helps to bring **regeneration**. Like the olive branch, she carries with her the promise of something new, inspiring those around her always to step up.

There are, of course, times when it is hard for Olive to step up, herself. Her consciousness is centred in the heart, and Olive's heart may have been wounded once too often. In her need for protection, Olive may have erected barriers around her heart, not only locking in the bitterness of her experience, but causing her to feel **unsupported** and alone. Magenta's quality of **passionate tenderness** will help to draw out the bitterness and heal the wounds. Olive may have a propensity to become a little too **rigid** in her thinking. Magenta's breadth and depth of understanding will help her, at times like this, to soften a bit, and broaden her view. Another aspect of Olive's psychology is that she might be given to the occasional **abuse of power**, allowing the concerns of her own ego to dominate the larger issues. Magenta, too, has the capacity to access considerable personal power if he chooses to use it; but his consciousness is more likely to remain centred within a spiritual as well as an unconditionally loving place; from this place, he can help to bring Olive back to the most positive use of her energies. Olive's fundamental **generosity** will make her quick to offer the olive branch, doing her part in restoring the peace.

Magenta, the passionate **idealist**, wants to bring heaven to earth; he wants to heal the whole world. The force of reality may at times be overwhelming for Magenta; in his disillusionment, he gives in to **despair**. Something of an **all-or-nothing** man, Magenta may opt for nothing when the larger plan seems unattainable. Olive, being better grounded, can help to bring his attention back to the details. She can help him to put his feet firmly on the earth and move forward, one step at a time.

Magenta is **unconditional** in the love he offers; always caring, he is generous to the point where he is worn to a shred. Olive may be a little more **realistic**: she knows not only her own limitations, but also his. Olive's heart energy, in health, is strong and free-flowing, but it is tempered with **discrimination** and **reason**: from this Magenta may well have a lot to learn. A trait they share is the preparedness to sacrifice their own desires if the need arises. Olive has the capacity to overcome the sometimes strident voice of her personal will when she sees that its interests are in conflict with the larger issues of the world around her. Her clear thinking in this regard may help Magenta, whose habit of self-sacrifice may be so deep as to over-ride the need for discrimination. Magenta holds in potential the gift of being **appropriate** and **precise** in his response to the situations which life offers him; Olive, with regard to this matter of self-sacrifice, however, may remind him of his need to access this quality rather than allow himself to become depleted in his service to others.

These two are likely always to be busy. They are not great party-goers. Always deeply involved in the manifold projects of their life, both separately and together, they put a high value on their time. Olive, easily claustrophobic, prefers to relax by finding peace and space; Magenta's ability to relax is not perhaps his strongest quality, but he is more likely to manage it on his own than in the middle of a crowd.

Olive Green and Magenta are both colours of great complexity. Olive Green has the capacity to bridge thinking and feeling: to bring reason into emotion and feeling into thought. This is how she achieves balance. Magenta has a highly developed sense of **divinity**; so highly developed, in fact, that he would sometimes much rather be in heaven than on earth. Nevertheless, when Magenta stays on an even keel, he is a wonderful bridge between the two dimensions, harnessing the full force of his energy and passion to the pursuit and the sharing of spiritual truth. Just as Olive brings the freshness of regeneration and a new season, so Magenta, like Beethoven, Schubert, or many artists, may be an inspired thinker or artist way ahead of his time.

Olive may, from time to time, be exasperated by Magenta's propensity to space out; Magenta may find Olive too obsessive about the office work or the washing up; but, in general, they are well equipped to find a harmonious balance. Between them active doers and thinkers, these two will never stagnate.

VIOLET AND YELLOW

His predominant colour choice is Yellow; hers is Violet. Like all complementary pairs, this means that in some respects they will complement each other's natures and complete one another, each having some of what the other lacks. They may, too, need to learn to respect and work with one another's shortcomings.

Yellow is **bright** and **happy**: all sunshine and laughter. He is probably an **individualist** as well. He is a **quick thinker** and likes to do his own thing. This is fine until his own thing conflicts with what someone else needs, when Yellow may continue to push on forward regardless of anyone else. In some respects Violet is perhaps a little more mature. She is more universal in her awareness; she sees the wider plan. She may be better at accommodating Yellow's wishes than he is at making space for hers. Violet, on the other hand, may be a little bit too **universal**. She very easily takes on the burdens of others and then becomes despondent. In fact, she is quite liable to bouts of **depression**. Always ready with a joke or a drink, Yellow will need to come in and lighten her up. Yellow, **intellectually** so **active**, is always full of new ideas. Some of these will probably work well; but if he learns to run them by Violet before rushing ahead, she will give them the deeper thought they often need. Yellow, however, with all his ideas, might also leave unfinished projects lying around, because his mind has gone on to something new. It may sometimes be Violet who finds herself picking up his loose ends and tying them all together.

Left to herself, Violet might quite easily feel **lonely**; with Yellow around, there will always be people coming and going. Violet may also need Yellow to goad her into action: she may be the equivalent of the old one who has seen it all, and who may find it hard at times to summon a sense of enthusiasm. It is Yellow's youthful **eagerness** that fires him with the energy to spark up new projects. Yellow, however, sometimes suffers from dreadful **anxiety** and **tension**. Usually so **cheerful** and **optimistic**, he can forget this when his worries get the better of him. Violet, here, might feel to him like his guardian angel as she builds a bridge over his troubled waters, pouring oil over them and reminding him of other dimensions beyond the only ones he can immediately see. Violet, although herself liable to periods of **depression**, has the sense to know that worry and anxiety sap the marrow from our bones. Knowing, if she is wise, that laughter leaves us much more energised than a fountain of tears, she will help Yellow to unwind by sitting down with him and watching a funny film. Her energy, in fact, is very much one of healing and service. Her ideal is to **bring heaven to earth**; so that any way in which she can make things better will be a source of immense satisfaction for her. She will watch with contentment as Yellow lets go of his fear and confusion and retrieves his dynamism. He is grateful for her **depth** and her **sound judgment** which backs and reassures him at the times when he doubts his own. She is grateful, at the times when her idealism takes her off into the realms of **fantasy**, for his ability to see clearly and practically and to bring her back down to earth.

There might be periods when Yellow finds Violet a bit **heavy**; and others, when Violet finds Yellow too **superficial**. Perhaps, when Yellow turns on the TV or the radio for the tenth time that day, Violet might need to know there is somewhere else she can go. She may want to set aside a special space for herself: for meditation, reading, quiet relaxation – whatever is her particular way. Yellow, absorbed in his next project, is unlikely to interfere. Sometimes, though, he may want to be active when she needs to be passive. Yellow, fired up by enthusiasm, and sometimes by an over-active ego, may occasionally embark on a **power trip**. If Violet is in a calm state of mind, this will not ruffle her feathers. But there are times, too, when Violet feels a need to **control** others; this might sometimes lead to deadlock.

Violet cannot resist the opportunity to **sacrifice** herself for others; though, simultaneously, she may feel maddened by this trait in herself. It is Yellow who can help her to see when this characteristic is helpful and when it is not, enabling her to gain a surer sense of her own individual nature and value. As it is Yellow who at other, less aware, times may unwittingly ignore Violet's needs altogether,

her ability to overcome the call of her ego for the greater good may come in very useful in the matter of keeping the peace between them.

With a bit of sensible negotiation from time to time, Yellow and Violet can co-exist in a way that is stimulating and supportive to both of them. They can help each other to grow through their weaknesses, support one another through times of sadness and difficulty, harness and develop together their greatest skills, and have a lot of fun.

INDIGO AND GOLD

Here is a royal couple: he with his love of deep Blue and she with her joyful appreciation of Gold. Jane Austen would have had fun with these colours in the creation of Mr. Darcy and Eliza Bennet: Indigo as the archetypal pride, Gold as prejudice. Indigo, all **dignity** and **honour**, is a highly **responsible** character. He does, however, tend to be rather serious. Gold, with her **ready wit** and **humour**, and perhaps the only one around with the **courage** to tease him, is always happy to liven things up.

Indigo prides himself on his **independence** of spirit, which is very real. He is also, however, someone of great **passion** and **depth**: once committed to his golden companion, he will give her his all. Gold has a **strength** of her own: like Indigo, she is intelligent. No-one can pull the wool over the eyes of either of this pair: each in their different way, they have the capacity to see far beyond the surface of things. Gold has the **wisdom**, and the subtlety, to bring out the best in Indigo. She knows intuitively when he needs companionship; but she understands, too, his need for privacy. In her balanced state, Gold will have no difficulty in respecting this.

There may be times, however, when Gold suffers bouts of deep **irrational fears**. Her formidable powers of reason are called in to no effect. It is at times like these that she will look, with gratitude and relief, to Indigo and thank her lucky stars, and him, for his unfathomable **calm**. Yet, at other times, this very calm may drive her mad: fired up with the **excitement** of a new idea, Gold hopes for Indigo's similar response. Indigo's dispassionate assessment, his **vision** which sees immediately further than hers, may well encourage him to consider the full picture rather than go along with Gold's passion. Gold, whose nature is very **companionable**, may feel Indigo's response like a wet blanket. Gold, however, never indulges for long in a state of frustration or resentment: tending to live in the moment, she will soon find something else to be happy about.

Gold has a sense of **value**: she appreciates all that is beautiful; she treasures her own possessions and respects those of other people; and she has a fierce loyalty to the people she loves. One of the challenges in Gold's life may be to find a similar dedication to herself and her *own* value. Gold may, at times, experience **deep self-doubt**; this can rock not only her confidence but her sense of purpose. Indigo can be of great assistance to her in enabling her to find her own centre: with his natural sense of **independence** and strength, he knows that she, too, contains her own wisdom, her own inner teacher, and he can help her to re-establish her connection with herself.

Indigo has a tendency to become **obsessive**. Pouring all the force of his energy into one channel, he is deeply satisfied when the outcome is successful, but he rumbles with frustration when he is not getting results. Gold has a natural tendency to be more broadly based: "I am not a great reader, and I have pleasure in many things" remarked Eliza Bennet sharply to an adversary. Gold can harness this gift in teaching Indigo not to put all his mental and emotional eggs into one basket. Left to himself, Indigo might work day and night for a week; he is fortunate in the choice of his Gold friend, who will entice him to look at the sunset, smell the flowers, and eat his meals. Indigo, too, can be a little **pompous**. With **pride** constantly lurking around Indigo's corner, he has need of Gold's reminder not to be over-earnest about himself. He is not easy to tease: Indigo's presence, often striking and powerful, inspires **respect** and even awe. In Gold, he has met his match; she never takes him as seriously as he is inclined to take himself.

Indigo and Gold can both be stubborn. Eliza Bennet's youthful conviction that she knew all the answers was as great a hurdle as was Darcy's pride. Part of the challenge for this pair will be to find a compromise when each is convinced that they are right. There may be difficulty, too, in Indigo's obsessiveness in the context of the scattiness which Gold can sometimes display: if she leaves papers lying around or constantly forgets the washing, the **meticulous** and somewhat **controlling** Indigo may want to scream. Both of these colours have a depth and a density which can make them, as long as they work in harmony, a powerful team.

Gold has a natural **curiosity** and a great desire to understand. Quite **impulsive**, she will delve into issues which may equally be personal or general, and then become overwhelmed with **confusion**. Indigo has a capacity for very deep seeing and thinking. When he harnesses this for Gold's benefit, he helps her to come to a new place of much clearer understanding. Indigo recognises in Gold the strength and the wide potential which she has often not seen for herself; he takes delight in polishing and refining her Golden essence. Indigo's love for Gold is enhanced by a deep sense of pride in this great treasure.

BLUE AND ORANGE

He cannot get enough Blue; she goes for Orange (or maybe, in your case, the other way round). She is up for anything **new** and **exciting**; he likes to **stay** with what he knows. Blue is the **conservative** and the **conservator**; Orange, whose energy is much more **explosive**, feels safe beside his strong protective energy. If Orange has lost her passport or her keys, the odds are that Blue will know where they are. Blue is both **dependable** and **independent**; in this way, he has something to teach Orange, who can scarcely survive a day on her own. Flamboyantly social, Orange loves company. More than this, she **needs** company. She is, in fact, highly susceptible to states of **dependency** or **co-dependency**. She needs others and she likes to feel invaluable to them. She thrives on the stimulus of those around her; her **effervescence** and her sense of fun make her the life and soul of the party. This can be difficult for Blue, who, as much as she wants her party, needs time on his own. Blue is very happy, as often as not, in the quiet of his own home with his favourite music and a good book. There may be times when Blue needs to hone his potentially strong **communication** skills in order to convey to Orange that his need for periods of **quiet peaceful** activity, or even silence, are purely his own and not a rejection of her. Orange has something of a tendency to measure her value in terms of other people's response to her; Blue, not having this need, is more likely to be his own master.

Blue, however, is subject to periodic attacks of **the Blues**. At these times, he may forget his normal self-sufficiency and suffer grave **loneliness**. Orange has the capacity here to **lighten** and raise his spirits. Not only does she bring him her **joy** and essential **optimism**; Orange also has gifts of deep **insight** which can make her a most understanding and sympathetic companion. She is also a great **lover**. Her **affection**, together with her frank **enjoyment of sex** as a joyful form of communication, melts the ice of Blue's loneliness. Blue is a cool ray, even cold;

there may be many circumstances where he needs the warmth of Orange. Orange, on the other hand, may on occasion get a little overheated; she may then need Blue to cool her down and restore her equilibrium. Orange is **emotional**; while she sometimes needs the calming influence of her peaceful Blue companion whose mental faculty is generally master of his emotions, there may be times when Blue's weakness is his **inability to show his feelings**. Strong and clear in the communication of his thoughts, Blue may hold his emotions too severely in check, leaving him apparently **rigid** and **cold**. Since, in reality, it is more likely that he feels isolated and at a loss to know how to express emotions which are quite strong, his choice of Orange as his companion is a wise one. She cannot fail to show her feelings: they are expressed in her laughter and her tears, her **body language** and the expressions on her face. If no-one else reaches him, she will.

Blue is essentially **peaceful**, but this, like all qualities, may from time to time sway out of balance. At these times, he may want peace at any price. On such occasions, his "anything for a quiet life" philosophy may cause him to duck important issues. Orange, who is not frightened of emotions, and may even enjoy a good fight now and again, will encourage him to speak out. But Orange, too, and in a very different context, may need to find a way to speak out. The choice of Orange often indicates that there has been some kind of deep **shock** or **trauma** in her life. In some cases, this is so severe that she has felt a kind of paralysis ever since the event. Blue, with his protective quality of peace and calm, can help to **soothe** her. Part of his strength, too, lies in his skills of communication; in helping Orange to express what it is that has traumatised her, he can help her to move through the experience and let it go. If Orange were left to cope with this on her own, such letting go might be almost impossible for her. It is possible that Orange may have suffered sexual abuse, or other abuse of trust; Blue has the potential to restore that **trust** and increase her **faith**.

Blue's wish to steer clear of a group may sometimes have its roots in a dislike of any kind of **authority** or challenge. His painful experiences of authority in the past may have made it hard for him to accept full **responsibility** for himself. In keeping away from group situations, he is avoiding the difficult issue of confronting some of the challenging aspects of himself, or of speaking his own truth. Orange can help him here to recognise and harness the social aspect of his nature. Another difficulty for Blue may be something of a tendency to escape into **abstractions**, living in a dreamland and **evading reality**. Orange has little problem in keeping her two feet on the ground, or at least one of them at a time; she will soon remind Blue where he is. In fact, Orange thoroughly enjoys the physical experience of being on earth: while Blue is thinking, she is dancing. Orange is **spontaneous**: this can be a lively stimulus to the conservatism and the sobriety of Blue. While Blue is living in the past or the future, Orange is firmly in the moment. While Orange is inside listening to a rock group, Blue is outside listening to the birds. While she may be drunk, he is probably sober. Orange may feel grateful that one of them has kept a clear head.

While Orange is physically active, Blue tends to be more passive. On a spiritual level, however, Blue is likely to be quite active. A thinker and someone drawn to meditation and contemplation, Blue has a universal consciousness and a deep desire to **communicate peace**. Blue may at times be joined in this by his Orange companion: always given to extremes, the intense nature of Orange may cause her to relinquish the physical material world as she finds a deeper joy, even bliss, through the way of meditation and prayer. If Orange takes this up, however, it will be with a light and **joyful** touch. One of Blue's weaknesses is his tendency to be rather **over-serious**. Orange can be relied upon, in most situations, not only to see the joke but to create it. While Orange's joy and love of life are a good balance for Blue's sober tendencies, there are times when Orange allows her sense of fun to run out of hand. The laughter may turn to **hysteria**; she may no longer know whether this is humour or grief, and Blue's steadying influence can be called in to save her from exhaustion.

Blue and Orange have the capacity to be very good friends. Though they may appear on the surface to be worlds apart, their differences are wonderfully complementary. Once they have understood their sometimes contrasting needs, they can nurture and support each other and find the deepest joy in one another's company.

TURQUOISE AND CORAL

Here is another pair rich in shared resources. He is Coral; she is Turquoise. The coral organism thrives in those Turquoise seas where the sun shines hot and long. In health, these two share a love of life which makes them spontaneous and creative. Different but alike, these two are both very sensitive.

Coral tends to be the more **private** of the pair. Frightened of the wounds he might suffer if he were to bare his soul, Coral will keep his feelings **hidden away**. He has quite a **dependent** nature, however; so that, once he feels secure in his relationship with Turquoise, he will hold nothing back from her. While he will give her everything he has, he also needs to feel that she knows him and understands everything about him. This may feel rather stifling for Turquoise, who has something of a need for **freedom**. Once Coral understands the need for Turquoise to come and go, he will learn to trust her to return. Coral's fear, in seeing Turquoise so happily absorbed in her own pursuits, is that he needs her more than she needs him. This may, to some extent, be the case; but Turquoise – if she is wise – will convince Coral that, while her need for him may not be overwhelming, her love for him is very deep.

Turquoise, with her freedom-loving, **expansive** nature, may sometimes be a little **abstract** in the way she lives. Gifted with a natural ability to communicate with great feeling on a wide scale, she may be stronger in conveying her ideals to others than she may always be in grounding these within her own life. A **philanthropist** and something of a philosopher, she may occasionally be bored by the practical demands of those who call on her time. More likely to be a lecturer or a painter than a counsellor or a nurse, she may be more impassioned by ideas about life and love than by the practice of them in stopping for her neighbour. In this, she can learn from Coral, who feels very **deeply bound** to those close to him. Coral's tremendous warmth gives him a rare **empathy** with those he cares about: he feels their every pain and joy and will stop at nothing in response to those who need him. In fact, Turquoise, in her turn, may occasionally need to remind Coral to find a little detachment for the sake of his self-preservation.

Coral's difficulty, as is so often the case with very sensitive people, is in gaining a real sense of his own **value**. Coral will easily elevate others, putting them on a pedestal, and perceive them as being superior to him in every way. This renders Coral very **vulnerable** to the pains of unrequited love. Coral may well have fallen in love with a whole chain of highly unsuitable people, most of whom have been quite unavailable to return this love, or even to notice it. Coral is quite likely to fixate on one person and convince himself that this is the only possible companion for him. Turquoise, with her natural sense of **freedom** and **independence**, has another quality which can help Coral in this situation. Turquoise is a **seeker**; her constant questing after personal truth and a higher purpose may encompass a much wider picture than just the personal details of her own life; and it can be turned towards her Coral friend. With the help of Turquoise, Coral may learn to see himself more clearly and to value himself more deeply. He may discover, too, the joy of reaching out a little wider and broadening his experience.

At other times, it may, of course, be Turquoise who needs the help. Turquoise, like Blue, is approaching the cooler end of the spectrum: Coral, near the other end, is the warm hearth. Turquoise, so open, so keen to express the observations of her **heart**, may have suffered much of her life from what she has experienced as a lack of opportunity to do so. It may well be that Turquoise has cultivated her **independence** in response to the feeling that she is **on her own**; that the listening ear she could have done with was never really there. She may be grateful for the strength of Coral's affection, which pulls her to ground and offers her the safety and warmth she never had in the past.

While Turquoise has the ability to **communicate creatively** and widely, Coral has a strong **sense of community**. While Coral is the fire, Turquoise is the breeze which fans the flame. When Coral is the inspiration, Turquoise may be the vehicle which gives it movement and form. Working together, these two can be a creative pair. Both blessed with a deep sense of **beauty** and **grace**, they can both nurture the beauty in nature and create it in their own lives.

Coral, similarly to Orange, may have experienced **abuse** or **shock**. Turquoise can be called in here to soothe the trauma and help Coral to separate himself from the experience. Where Coral has put the lid on his shock, locking it in to fester, Turquoise can gently prize open the lid and set free the pain. When Turquoise, in her perpetual search for perfection, has lost her grounding in a sea of ideas, Coral can lead her gently back to reality, and help her to be in the physical world. At other times, it may be that the flow of Turquoise's **creative force** is **blocked** up like a dam, until she feels tight with tension. She will be glad of Coral's quiet **warmth**, which supports her just the way things are until she can relax again and move back into the flow.

While Coral may from time to time be alarmed by Turquoise's apparent **absence of mind** (which comes not from any lack of care, but from her tendency to lean towards abstractions and ideas rather than to be fully present in the moment) and Turquoise in her turn may occasionally feel irritated by Coral's lack of adventure, they are nonetheless well-matched. Coral's energy is a beautiful balance of **wisdom** and **love**. In health and harmony, Coral is a rare jewel of a companion, especially perhaps to Turquoise, whose essential quality is not so dissimilar. While she may not always manage to live up to it, Turquoise personifies an ideal: the creative communication of the heart. In balance, the heart of Turquoise is an open channel through which the Coral fount of love and wisdom may flow. Together, they have the resources for great happiness and fulfillment.

• • • • •

These six pairs of complementary colours are examples which most clearly demonstrate the potential within our colour choices to unearth the gifts in our relationships. They are useful because they show a clear polarity as well as a complementarity within their relationships. But it is important to recognize that this is not a limited, finite state of affairs. All colours have some kind of relationship with all the others. Blue and Red can show the obvious contrast between one who is focussed on the abstract and the divine and another who is firmly centred in the physical world. The polarity within Blue and Pink might point to male-female issues. Case histories within the next few chapters will serve to illustrate many of the possibilities offered by other combinations of colours. It is beyond the scope of one book to illustrate in any detail the dynamics between all the possible combinations; but from the information offered, you will soon find it quite easy to look at your own colour choices in combination with a loved one, and to contemplate many of the lessons and gifts contained within them.

The colour wheel serves as a constant reminder that within many colours are hidden others; so that, for example, while Violet and Yellow have been cited as clear complementary opposites, there are others which can be seen as near neighbours. Magenta, for example, is very close to Violet, so there is a certain amount to be discovered within the relationship of Magenta to Yellow. The skill, in contemplating ourselves and one another through colour, is to discover not only those gifts and strengths which are easily found, but also the opportunities which lie beneath our differences, waiting to bring a new degree of warmth, intimacy and love into our partnerships.

The practice of counselling through a person's choice of colour is based, like all holistic therapies, on the understanding that every human being is unique. It also stands out from other methods by its unique feature: that everyone coming to it chooses their own colours, thus taking responsibility for themselves and their own path. Nothing is imposed from the outside. A colour counsellor is unlikely, in most circumstances, to offer advice on the colour needed, but will rather offer the client the choice; except in a few situations – such as shock, grief or impending birth, for example – where a colour has been picked so universally as to become almost a specific remedy.

We can never predict exactly what another person will choose. However, in order that you may now check on how much you have absorbed of some of the key concepts associated with each colour, you can enjoy a simple check-up, or quiz. The questions asked merely suggest scenes which pinpoint concepts with a fairly clear, straightforward connection to one colour or another, bringing to mind a few key words such as joy, shock, passion, grief and so on. For the sake of simplicity, they also concentrate more on questions of immediate colour needs than on the deeper and more complex ones of a person's essential quality. There are no hard and fast answers to these questions: merely answers that are suggested on the grounds that the problem may point up a clear and specific issue. You may always have a different opinion than the one suggested in the list of possible answers.

A Check-up

I Adam has just heard that he's got the job. There were 120-odd candidates, so he had not dared to give free rein to his hopes. As he celebrates that evening, a friend invites him to choose the colour he likes the most. Which is more probable?

   a Magenta   **b** White   **c** Gold

2 Camilla is preparing for the birth of her child, which could happen any day. After a difficult experience the first time, she is a little nervous. Her friend, a colour therapist, wants to help Camilla to keep calm. If, in this case, the therapist is keen to bring Camilla an immediate remedy, which is the most likely colour that she will offer her?

   a Red   **b** Blue   **c** Olive Green

3 Sally's friends begin to notice a gradual change in her. She has always been relied on to share a joke and keep people smiling, but she is not quite herself these days until she has had at least a drink or two. If she were offered a colour selection at this time, her first choice might be:

a Pale Blue   **b** Orange   **c** Violet

4 Stephen and Jessica, after two years of living together, have been fighting. Stephen wants desperately to calm things down, and find a way for both of them to reconnect with the love he knows is there. He seeks support from a colour therapist during this crisis while they are trying to find their way back to each other. Stephen is attracted towards:

a Yellow   **b** Indigo   **c** Pink

5 Dorothy has come for colour counselling following the death of her husband. After forty years of marriage and his slow death by cancer, she is finding the change quite hard to adjust to. She is likely to be drawn towards:

a Pink   **b** Gold   **c** Violet

6 Marjorie has fallen desperately in love with her tutor, a married man with several young children. She has no intention of having an affair with him, and does not anyway suppose that this man is even particularly aware of her, but the situation is causing her great pain. She feels attracted to the colour:

a Coral   **b** White   **c** Indigo

7 Gordon, an ambitious businessman, is about to make a takeover bid for a company competing very closely with his. He might show a preference for:

a Blue   **b** Turquoise   **c** Red

8 Michael is an overworked doctor; Susan, his wife, goes between her job as a teacher and as mother of their three young children. As both begin to sense the strain on their marriage Susan, who is beginning to suffer from a sense of claustrophobia, goes for colour counselling. She is particularly attracted at this time in her life to:

a Violet   b Green   c Gold

9 Hugh, an intense, nervous, slightly hyper-active student, has just been called for interview at a highly acclaimed university. A boy from a severely dysfunctional family, he has long made this his life's ambition. A probable choice of colour for him at this time might be:

a Turquoise   b Gold   c Red

10 Nicola is in the full flush of pregnancy with her first baby. Her husband, very proud and devoted to her, wants to cherish her in every way he can. He sends her for a colour counselling session to encourage her to spend time on herself. She is most likely to be drawn to:

a Green   b Yellow   c Pink

11 Nancy has been invited to partake in a TV chat show which will feature the music therapy work she does with autistic children. The colour which might be likely to attract her attention at this time may be:

a Turquoise   b White   c Red

12 After nearly thirty years in full-time nursing, June has just retired. In order to be nearer to her daughter, she has also moved to an area of the country she hardly knows. To help her through this change, her daughter suggests colour counselling. A possible favourite for June might be:

a Olive Green   b Violet   c Coral

13 Helen has recently suffered a major breakdown. She has been too ill to consider returning to her previous job; she still feels weak and empty, and she has no idea what she hopes for. Her friend sends her for some colour therapy. A colour which may attract Helen at this time is:

    a Orange   **b** Turquoise   **c** White

14 Jane has just, after years of struggle, made her escape from a relationship in which she felt completely controlled. She and Luke had shared a very small flat, and Luke had tried to prevent her from any activity which did not involve him. Panting for breath, she came with relief to look at colours. A likely first choice would be:

    a Indigo   **b** Pale Green   **c** Magenta

15 Heather has lived for years on her own. She supports herself, with difficulty, by small-scale journalism. Her few relationships have ended in tears; her novels have been turned down by scores of publishers. She keeps on writing. A possible colour choice for her at this time might be:

    a Pink   **b** Olive Green   **c** Gold

16 James, aged 13, is recovering with a foster family from his experiences at the hands of a drunken violent father who has made frequent visits day and night to his mother's house to beat her up. James has an obsessive need to go around the house at night checking that the doors are locked. A colour choice which might be especially likely for him is:

    a Pale Yellow   **b** Magenta   **c** White

17 David and June have been fairly peacefully married for thirty years. June's parents have always been particularly demanding and difficult, and David has found their visits very stressful. June's father has now suffered a stroke and there has been no available alternative but for both parents to spend at least a few months staying in June and David's house. It is David who comes for help through colour counselling, having found the radical onslaught on their privacy and way of life almost intolerable. He might well be drawn to:

a Blue   b Pink   c Pale Violet

18 Sophie and John had been married for a couple of years and were finding it increasingly difficult to communicate with each other, John apparently relating only to his music which absorbed him for hours and days at a time in his studio. When Sophie persuaded John to consult a colour therapist, the colour which most appealed to John was:

a Coral   b Indigo   c Green

19 Mark and Julia met when they both became involved in the project of restoring a large garden. They shared a great love for plants and for colour, and looked to colour counselling for general interest and for confirmation about the direction of their relationship. They found that the colours which attracted them the most were very similar. The most probable one as a favourite choice was:

a Violet   b Pale Yellow   c Green

20 Daisy was a secretary in a cosmetics company; she was suffering a great sense of futility and frustration. She gained no fulfilment from the work, and always made excuses to avoid the social gatherings to which the other girls invited her. When she sought help through colour to overcome her feeling of depression, she is likely to have found herself drawn to:

a Gold   b Orange   c Magenta

Suggested Answers

1 Gold – he was likely to be feeling joy and the release of tension.

2 Blue – one of the most soothing rays.

3 Orange – it often points to addictve behaviours. Alternatively, Violet is healing and transformative, and has the capacity to bring the necessary balance and calm for her to seek the truth of her inner situation.

4 Pink – this helps to create a softer and more loving atmosphere.

5 Violet – this colour has strong associations with grief, with changes and the ending of cycles.

6 Coral – this colour often comes up when there is unrequited love.

7 Red – his current concerns were to do with material and earthly issues.

8 Green – she is likely to be feeling a need for space.

9 Gold – this seems probable because of his intense and rather nervous disposition, though Turquoise might help him to open his communication channel for a successful interview!

10 Pink – she is probably feeling very much loved; "in the Pink".

11 Turquoise – the context requires clear and heartfelt communication on a wide scale.

12 Violet – this move is likely to be a profound change for her.

13 White – people choose this colour when they feel washed out. On the other hand Orange would help her through the shock of this experience.

14 Pale Green – the yearning for space was probably quite intense.

15 Olive Green – she has suffered bitter rejections and has kept batting on.

16 Pale Yellow – the fear is likely to be intense. Another possible choice might be Magenta, showing his great need for "Divine" love in the absence of any earthly love.

17 Pale Violet – for extreme change, and also for healing him and enabling him to accept this act of service.

18 Indigo – his solitary lifestyle and his intensity might well indicate this colour.

19 Green – their love of nature and open spaces, and perhaps their current state of harmony.

20 Magenta – her depression and loneliness combined with the search for meaning and purpose might draw her towards this colour.

PART THREE

COLOUR AS A MIRROR

And I saw another mighty angel come down from heaven, clothed with a cloud: and a rainbow was upon his head, and his face was as it were the sun, and his feet as pillars of fire.

REVELATIONS 10:1

chapter 9

THE FLAME

There is a flame within me that has stood
Unmoved, untroubled through a mist of years...
John Spencer Muirhead
The Jewel in the Lotus

I n this chapter, you can start to look at the colour you have already chosen, via your colour spectrum cards, as your most favourite of all those offered. Before you do this, try to forget for a moment all the information you may have just read, look once more at the selection of colours available, and satisfy yourself that the colour you have chosen is the one to which you are most drawn. It is your body, your heart, your intuition that is choosing this colour: not your mind, which may already, through the last few chapters, have acquired a few thoughts about the colours that you like, or dislike. Are you confident that you would be happy to have this colour around you for quite a long time? Make sure you feel reasonably satisfied that you would live happily with this first colour choice. Don't worry if it takes you a little while to decide.

Before proceeding to study the implications of your first choice, it would be good if you were now to select a second colour card. Ideally you can then continue on to choose a third and then a fourth colour, as it works best to make a complete selection at any one time. You will, however, need to allow yourself some time to digest the contents of the next few chapters, which will take you on quite a journey of exploration. Your colours once selected, you may wish to refer at once to the Personal Selection Charts on pages 185–187 in order to make a note of them. This will enable you to work at your own pace through the process that will follow.

Reading Your Colours

Having chosen the colours you prefer, you can now begin to bring the insights into their messages given in Part Two to a formula for reading this choice of colours, if possible alongside the selection of a friend or loved one. These chapters will guide you through a process which has its roots in the philosophy and practice of Aura-Soma, the school of colour therapy already mentioned in Chapter 1. This method has been tried and tested with millions of clients world-wide, for something approaching two decades. I used the Aura-Soma system for some years, with thousands of students and clients in many different cultures, before adapting it for specific application within the context of relationships. The Aura-Soma method for interpretation of your colour selection is a four-step one:

Colour 1: reflects something of your fundamental quality;
Colour 2: speaks particularly of issues which have challenged and
   tested you in the past;
Colour 3: offers a readout of your current state of mind and heart;
Colour 4: suggests the direction in which you are headed.

This formula has been found to apply universally. The method suggested here, for pairs of individuals in a number of contexts, has been developed from this system.

The colour which has the deepest and longest-lasting appeal for you is the one that reflects something of your quality, or essence. It shows a lot about where you are coming from. It offers all sorts of insights both into yourself as an individual, and into the dynamics of your intimate relationship, if you are looking at colour as a couple. The first colour choice of each of you, as individuals, is referred to within Aura-Soma teaching as your "soul colour". The colour indicates, above all, something of your *essential quality*: the still point at the centre of the storm of life, as it were, which remains true to itself while all that is around you may be in a perpetual process of movement and change. So, this first part of your selection helps you to recognise yourself in a different way from before; to see the spirit or flame, the "real you", at the core of yourself, that somehow or other remains steady and firm no matter how much your circumstances may alter; and which you take with you into your intimate relationships.

ESSENCE

If you are choosing colours with a partner, you can first look at what your initial choice says about each of you separately. You can begin to acknowledge some of your hidden, or sometimes less hidden, qualities. Suppose you have chosen Yellow: this colour speaks of your lively mind, your sunny, fun-loving nature which may render you a frequent guest at parties, as you are probably well aware. But it may simultaneously alert you to some of your less conscious tendencies: occasionally to ride roughshod, for instance, over the needs of others when you are 100% focussed on a particular goal; or to get caught up in an overdose of anxiety so that, just when you need to think clearly, you turn into a bag of nerves. Or, imagine that you have chosen Olive Green: this may speak of your stamina and persistence, your steady ability to balance feeling and thought, your gift for constantly looking at things with a mind fresh and alert, and your natural leadership qualities. Conversely, and at the same time, it might remind you of your need to find the trust to let go into life again after an experience of bitterness and hardship; perhaps it suggests that, while in your struggle to persist alone you have developed a great strength, you also need to cultivate an attitude which is more flexible.

Which colour have you chosen? What does this choice tell you about your *strengths*? What does it tell you about the areas where you need to pay *more attention*? Use the information given in Part Two to study the portrait, as it were, of the colour you have chosen first. Then use one of the Personal Selection Charts on pages 185–187 to make a note of those characteristics, the positive as well as those that present difficulties, which you recognise as belonging to you. In this way you can begin to build up your own personal case study.

If you are working jointly with another person, then when you have each taken a good look at your own colour and begun to assemble your respective charts, you can move on to fill in the joint chart and begin to see how your individual hues get along together. In other words, this first choice will give each of you the opportunity of taking a new look at one another. It hints at some of the ways in which you may have been drawn together through similarity, and at some of the ways in which you differ. It reminds you of the golden rule for good communication: to understand where the other person is coming from. Your colour choices at this point in the selection help you to do just that. If your partner is not interested in actively joining in, he or she may nevertheless be quite willing to tell you which of the colours shown attracts them the most. With the other person's consent, this gives you a tool to do much of the work yourself and have a lot of fun while you are at it. Once you have had a good look at these colours, there are several aspects about the dynamics in your relationship that can be looked at under specific headings.

BIRTH

We can look at any close relationship as something which, like the cycle of time in nature, has four seasons. The first colour choice corresponds to the first phase in this four-seasoned cycle of relationships: that of birth. Birth is a process which fills us with a sense of mystery and awe; and this is as true in the birth of a bond of love as it is in the birth of a baby. We can only very partially understand it. The essential mystery of its source remains intangible. If you have known your partner for a long time, then the contemplation of your first, separate choices of colour, and also of the way in which these combine or inter-relate, may help to bring you back to that sense of wonder that originally gave this friendship its unique value. It will prompt you to look at yourselves and one another through lenses that perceive more deeply, and with more compassion. It will enable you to look at the gift, and the complexity, of what you bring to one another and what you share in the outer world.

Sam and Anita

We looked earlier at Sam and Anita, who were encountering quite severe problems at the time that they came for advice. Anita's first choice was **Orange**; Sam's was **Violet**. On the face of it, these two colours show very little similarity to one another. This couple's first colours showed that, in many ways, these two were coming from very different places. And yet their individual colour choices also hinted at some of the ways in which they could support each other through their differences. Anita's "**Orange**" **vitality**, **passion** and **enthusiasm** had been a major factor in the very powerful attraction that the more sober and reserved Sam had felt towards her when they had met in Hong Kong. Sam's "**Violet**" temperament, which was **steadier** and much more **stable** than Anita's, with its quiet suggestion of **authority** and **strength**, had drawn Anita strongly towards him. It had been easy, through the subsequent period of breakdown in their communication, for Anita to forget about many aspects of Sam's nature that she had valued and loved at the outset. The first thing that these two colours reminded them both was that Anita was not the only one of the two with a passionate nature, particularly in regard to their emotions and their love life. Red is the quintessential colour to denote passion: Violet and Orange both contain the colour Red in fairly similar proportions. This suggests that one of the things that separated them was not Sam's absence of passion, but rather their *different expressions* of it.

Let's have a closer look at this so that you can throw some similar light on some of your own colours. Anita's Orange combines Red with Yellow. Sam's Violet combines Red with Blue. What does this tell you? It shows that Anita's constitution contains elements of Yellow, and a quick glance at **Yellow** offers us some immediate hints: **quick-thinking**, **vitality**, **happy-go-luckiness**, **self-centredness**, **fear**. And it shows that Sam's constitution contains elements of **Blue**, so here are some more hints: **independence**, **calm**, **quietness**, **protectiveness**, and possible **loneliness**.

Some contemplation of both their colours brought Anita and Sam each to look at one another in a new way, to notice afresh each other's strong qualities and to open up a path towards talking and listening to one another again. It also helped them to remember why they had been drawn to come together in the first place. Here is a quick checklist of some of the key words for the positive attributes of these two colours:

Orange:	Violet:
Extrovert, joyful, blissful, sociable, sexual, physical, spontaneous, deep insight, companionable.	*Balanced strength, quiet, sober, thoughtful, dedicated to service, contemplative, idealist, self-sacrificing, spiritually inclined, natural healer.*

A look at key words such as these was sufficient for Anita and Sam to get some kind of conversation started again. Sam had forgotten how much he enjoyed Anita's sense of exhilaration and fun, how much she sparked him off and showed him how to enjoy life; Anita had missed Sam's ability, when he had been prepared to listen to her, to show a deeper understanding of people, including her own family, than she sometimes had. He was also quick to find a broader perspective than she could in relation to work: her business ideas got off to a hopeless start without Sam's much more orderly, sober mind. This represents only the beginning of their journey into colour, but already they were in a position to see each other more clearly and with much more compassion than before. Eventually, they realised they had come close to falling in love all over again, but in a new, rooted and much less hazardous way.

A checklist of this sort, concentrating only on what is positive, can be a useful aid to a couple in affirming themselves and one another. Try it, first for yourself. Pick out those characteristics shown by your colour that you know are lying dormant somewhere inside, but which perhaps have not found the conviction to come out and express themselves. Use the relevant colour affirmations in Part Two, or create some of your own, using these key words, and place them in strategic places: on mirrors, and on the walls of your bedroom, kitchen or office. Remember that the more you believe in and value yourself, the more you will have to offer your partner (and everyone else in your life).

Rick and Maddi

Another couple, Rick and Maddi, were reminded through this first choice of colour of the magic of the moment when their relationship slipped over from one of tentative friendship to the recognition that something had happened that was new for both of them. Maddi was the only daughter of a woman whose husband had died while she was pregnant with her. She had grown up without any men around her, and had always felt shy in their presence. Maddi could relate to men as colleagues at work, but she was ill at ease whenever the boundaries looked as though they were about to extend into the personal field. Rick's first marriage had ended in a very sudden and hurtful way, several years before he joined the company where Maddi was employed. They worked together on several projects before Rick summoned the courage to ask Maddi out for an evening. Once he realised that for months she had been hoping, and not knowing how, to get together with him, the defences that Rick had erected around himself for some time began to dissolve. He soon noticed his old sense of fun returning and found himself gently teasing Maddi, who had never been lovingly teased in her life by anyone, let alone a man. Years later, after raising a handicapped child and encountering many other challenges together, Rick's choice of **Yellow** and Maddi's choice of **Turquoise** reminded each of them of their partner's particular quality that was always accessible, even when outer circumstances appeared, as they sometimes had done, to bury it alive.

If your relationship is still young, then the contemplation of these first colours will give a new dimension to the way you perceive each other. It will help you to understand what it is in each of you that has drawn you together, and to trust the value of what, together, you have birthed. The perception of this might remind you at various times in the future of the value of this choice; that, in spite of whatever problems you may encounter, this choice came from reality and truth. It goes without saying that not every intimate relationship is destined to be a deep and long-term one. There is no magic recipe for turning chalk and cheese into a velvety soufflé, and the challenge is sometimes to recognise when a relationship has no more potential to serve those involved. But if you are currently working on a partnership and have come thus far in reading this book, you can be pretty sure that there is plenty of reality and truth at the core of your connection, and that the trouble you are taking is worthwhile. If you have been together for a long time, it might be helpful to freshen things up by remembering not only how far you have come together, but also where you have both come from. Do you still notice each other with anything like the perception that you once did? Do you slip into taking one another for granted? Do you reinforce each other on a daily basis, rather than leaving this until some event reminds you to do so?

COMPLEMENTARITY

If you are working with a partner, how do your colours seem to fit together? Look at such things as their primary, secondary or tertiary nature. Above all, take great care at this moment to avoid slipping into judgment, either of yourself or of your partner. This is a habit deep in most of us, and particularly unhelpful if we are trying to hone our communication skills. The choice of a primary colour, for example, may indicate directness and strength of a sort, but also perhaps a certain tendency towards a single focus which may limit your vision in some directions. The choice of a tertiary colour, on the other hand, may suggest gifts of subtlety and sensitivity, but may also show that you are sometimes a little vague and hard to pin down. Look at the colour wheel. Do your colours come close to each other (e.g. Turquoise and Green, or Yellow and Gold)? This might indicate some strong similarities between you, but also subtle differences which may have caused difficulties when you have assumed that your partner automatically understands something that is clear to you, but which in fact (s)he perceives differently from you. Here is an extract from another couple's history to illustrate this:

Michael and Sophie

Michael and Sophie chose **Red** and **Magenta**, respectively. At first sight, these colours appear quite similar, which was exactly how Michael perceived them to be. They were both people who had been very energetic and enthusiastic in earlier years, and they had achieved a lot together in building up a beautiful home, comfortable wealth and several children. Yet Sophie had long felt depressed at the gulf between them. With her propensity to **think** a lot, and her natural tendency to **stand outside** many situations and feel **alone**, she could see the picture much more clearly, at present, than Michael could. She was frustrated by what she experienced as his simplistic assumptions that they were very happy, and well-suited to each other. Michael's **physical energy** and stamina remained high, and he had stayed focussed on **business**, where he was strong and successful. Sophie, on the other hand, was quite depleted at this time. She felt both unable to keep up with Michael's rather restless pace and distressed by the fact that he appeared not to notice that they scarcely ever really talked to each other; and also that he was similarly oblivious of the various difficulties experienced by their youngest daughter. This was also the classic case of "he wants sex; she wants love – and conversation". Magenta actually contains a high proportion of Red; yet it is a more complex energy, containing within it some of the features associated with Pink, and with Red, and with Violet. If Michael could bend away from the direct **simplicity**, and also the **stubbornness**, of his Red, he would begin to see that, once the difficulties between them were faced, they had the potential to support each other in lots of ways. For a start, Sophie had the inner resources to broaden and enrich his experience by raising his awareness beyond the workaday concerns of the material world. Michael quite quickly recognised this and acknowledged that this was just what Sophie had done throughout their marriage, whenever he had taken the trouble to respond to her. For another thing, they both knew not only how easily Sophie could become **over-concerned** for those around her and exhaust herself, but also her tendency to "**space out**" and get stuck in a world of ideas. She was much in need of Michael's counterbalancing, very practical energy, that lived in the here-and-now and brought her to ground.

As these two discussed their selection of colours, one of the first things they agreed was that, for the next month, they would put sex aside completely: each of them would contemplate the other one's first colour, as well as their own, and they would reinforce it through discussion as well as by other, practical means. They later reported that not four days had gone by before they were back in bed together. It doesn't have to take a lifetime to get things together again when both partners are getting some of their needs recognised!

HIGHER PURPOSE

What two people bring together in a close friendship is greater than the sum of their separate parts. This realisation can encourage you to look at the purpose of your relationship. In essence, this purpose is pretty similar in all those partnerships which have value and truth. It is to grow and expand together in the presence of something greater, and mysterious, which according to your creed you might call by many different names: the universe, the source, God, or whatever name you ascribe to your concept of divinity. Whatever name you give it, your relationship takes on purpose and meaning, and finds balance, in the presence of this third energy.

It is this commitment to a higher purpose in a relationship that helps the people within it to support each other in growing towards their *full potential*: "to become", in the words of M. Scott Peck, "the most of which they are capable" (*The Road Less Travelled*, M. Scott Peck, Random House).

> *Whatever name you give it, your relationship takes on purpose and meaning, and finds balance, in the presence of this third energy.*

How does your colour choice come together with that of your partner? What would happen if you mixed them together? Coral and Gold would come together as a gorgeous, subtler shade of Orange; Blue and Turquoise as some heavenly peacock colour. Exact complementary colours, on the other hand, are more likely to mix to a Brown sludge. If you don't happen to like the colour Brown, cheer up, as we return for a moment to some simple theory. Colours which are direct complementary opposites (Blue and Orange, for example; Magenta and Olive Green; or any others), if combined like paints on a palette, will always form some kind of Brown; and this is because, together, they contain all the three primaries in a fairly even balance. This is the first thing that any art student is likely to learn. Brown, not having an individual identity in relation to the rainbow spectrum, does not form part of the core language of colour. This is the reason why little coverage has been offered to this hue in many systems of colour therapy. If your colours were to combine to Brown, remember that this probably means that, between you, your colours contain a broad spectrum of possibilities, even though many of these may have remained hidden. Furthermore, Brown is not only very grounding, but also has its own associations as a colour of great fertility (the earth, autumn, leaves returning to nourish the next season's growth – and so on).

All this aside, complementary colours, along with their paler tints and darker shades, generally look very good when used together. Blue combines wonderfully with the pale Orange that is generally known as Peach; and think of Turquoise and Coral, Violet and Yellow, Indigo and Gold, Pink and Green. This is an asset when it comes to combining your "soul" colours in a practical way, such as within the décor in your home.

Angela and Desmond

The colours you have chosen help you to come to an understanding of the ways in which you can achieve the real growth that brings you nearer to your full potential, and to a living relationship with your spirit: that aspect of yourself which is in touch with why you came to be here at all. Angela and Desmond chose **Pink** and **Indigo**, respectively. Here is a neatly clear-cut and straightforward example: the colour formed by the combination of these is **Violet**. This new colour contains the energies of both the Pink and the Indigo, and it also transcends them. **Violet** is an energy of powerful **transformation** and **change**. It brings us into line with our purpose and our sense of **service** on earth. Angela had been adopted as a young baby and had grown up with a sense of vulnerability, and also a deeply buried but very powerful feeling of resentment towards the two natural children who had been born to her adopted parents later. She had felt frail, resentful, and insubstantial by turns in her childhood, but was also conscious of great gratitude towards her adoptive parents. The belief that she must always be grateful and display the "correct" emotions had stifled her and prevented her from achieving anything close to her full potential until, in her early thirties, she had met Desmond. Desmond's difficulty had more to do with the loneliness of growing up with an increasingly sick mother who had then died, leaving him in his late teens with a bewildered and grief-stricken father. Both Desmond and Angela had had plenty of opportunities to develop their powers of insight and observation, and the combination of their colours to form Violet confirmed their ability to offer each other the possibility of transmuting the pain and the difficulty of the past. In its place, they could nourish their strength, their understanding and their insight, and come to see more deeply what each of these difficult situations had taught them. In this way, they both became aware that they had come together as a profound healing force in each other's lives. Violet is the quintessential ray for healing on all levels.

BALANCING OF MALE AND FEMALE POLARITIES

The colour Violet is a useful illustration in another way: it combines the Blue energies of the masculine and the Pink of the feminine, and brings them into balance. This is a necessary task for all of us if we are ever to resolve the battle between the sexes. The division between the sexes is one of the most pressing polarities of our time, as well as the single most pressing issue within intimate relationships. John Gray has helped millions of people to confront the problem of the sexes through his metaphor of Mars and Venus (*Men are from Mars, Women are from Venus*, John Gray, Thorsons). We could extend this a little further and remind ourselves that both these planets revolve around the sun…. We could also remind ourselves of the bottom line: that, somehow or other, every one of us from everywhere has the most profound connection with light. Light has the radical ability to move us beyond this state of polarity and towards unity. As we move away from this age-long imbalance that has kept the masculine and feminine separate and apart, we discover that both energies are contained within us all: that the division is not a sharp one, but a spectrum. Some of us are nearer to one end and some to the other. Every human being is a balance of both forces: the yin and the yang, the cool and the warm, the feminine and the masculine, the intuitive and the rational.

When you begin to come to an inner balance of those male-female polarities within yourself, each partner can come to the other in the balanced fullness of his or her masculinity **and** femininity. The masculine force is archetypically that of the intellect, reason, structure and discipline: it is projective and relates to the outer aspect of ourselves and our experience. The feminine force is archetypically that of the intuition, the feelings, creativity and content: it relates to the inner aspect of things. Every one of us, whatever our physical gender, contains something of both these

> *Every human being is a balance of both forces: the yin and the yang, the cool and the warm, the feminine and the masculine, the intuitive and the rational.*

energies. This means that, in a balanced state, the man who is at ease with his own feminine aspect can truly meet the physical woman who is his partner; and similarly, the woman who is at one with her masculine side can meet the man she is with. In other words, when we are at ease with our own *inner* man or woman, we can sit comfortably with the *outer* man or woman. Ultimately, this is the only route by which partners will meet each other on equal terms.

Angela, in her **Pink** conviction that she must always be "**nice**", had found it very difficult to take hold of her strength and authority and deal squarely with her real emotions; in other words, she had not owned her masculine side. Desmond's choice of **Indigo** showed that, after losing his mother so young, he had suppressed his painful emotions and to some extent denied the *woman* inside himself, constructing a slightly **rigid**, **male structure** to make his life appear more predictable than it was ever likely to be. The colour Violet has a strong message here: through faith, reflection and understanding, this ray is able to bring deep healing to old wounds; it also addresses specifically the possibility of finding this much-needed inner balance between the masculine and feminine forces. These two people, though they would of course have challenges to face, would be able to offer one another great opportunities for the healing of childhood wounds and the growth that takes place when we feel supported.

COMMUNICATION

In the context of this deeper appreciation of your qualities and those of your partner, you can begin to build the foundations for a new level of communication between each other, which is founded on two essential features: *active listening*, and the *speaking of your truth*. As you come to an understanding of where your loved one is coming from, you are increasingly able to climb into his or her shoes, so that you are able to listen to one another with empathy: feeling rather than guessing at whatever it is that the other person needs to communicate. And, as the contemplation of your own essence or quality helps you to come to a new degree of appreciation of your own strengths as well as your limitations, you come into touch with your own inner truth. Once you are in touch with your own truth, you can communicate it. In the context of clarity and mutual respect, you can both listen and speak.

Communication is more than merely a function of the senses: it is a function of energy. Energy originates in light, and has its expression through colour. We glanced in Chapter 3 at the way that relationship involves an exchange of energy. When you are in the first flush of love, what you bring to each other is the positive aspect of all the colours that express what you are. In this abundant state, you are able to fill each other up in a flowing exchange of positive energy. To contemplate your colours is to come into contact with yourself in a new way, and this has immediate and positive effects on the quality of the energy field around you, even before you have harnessed any physical vehicles to bring a particular colour or colours into your energy field. It is possible, by endeavouring to live your life consciously, to make efforts to stay on the positive side of the qualities you possess. This helps you to continue the nurturing of the relationship and to keep the initial passion and communication alive. Colour is an invaluable ally in this.

The information contained within the colour is energy at another level; and as the light gently brings hidden aspects of yourself to your awareness, it dispels the fog; it helps you to overcome those obstacles in yourself that have hindered your growth, and creates an atmosphere within which communication becomes clearer and deeper. In recognising the more challenging aspects of the colours, or qualities, that you bring, you can begin to understand their cause so that you can overcome them. When two people work hand in hand to bring colour into their communications, their combined power is, of course, even greater.

There are many simple and practical means by which this communication can be steadily enhanced and reinforced and the energies of these colours thoroughly incorporated into daily life. The first step is to discuss with each other the way you feel about the insights that your colours reveal, both about yourselves individually and about your partner. Colour offers a unique gift when used in this way. As a "therapy", colour is *non-intrusive*. There is no-one outside yourself sticking labels on you, judging you in any way, or even offering you a remedy. It is because *you* choose the colours yourself that there is nothing imposed on you from outside, and any difficult issues they bring up are ones that some part of you already knows that you are ready to address.

Practical Use of *Soul* Colours

After this discussion of your colours with your partner, you can bring colour into your surroundings and your consciousness in all sorts of practical ways. The effort of paying attention to the ways in which these colours can be included in daily living is always well rewarded. You can offer each other your particular colours through small gifts and in little ways such as food, essential oils, flower essences and many others: you will find these substantially covered in Part Four. If you live together, then one of the most obvious methods you can use to bring these colours in as part of your permanent base is to include them in the décor and furnishing.

The first colour choice of either partner is best used in only relatively small amounts: however unconscious this fact may have been in the past, the colour affects you at a profound level and to have it in too many places and in too large doses can be a little unsettling. On the other hand, of all the colours you choose, this first one is the most likely to remain with you; whereas the second and subsequent ones are more likely to change. It is good to put this first choice of your colours within the entrance to the house: the front door, perhaps; a hall or passageway. Think of details such as the floor or the lampshades. Another good place is the main room, whether that is your kitchen/dining room or a separate sitting room. If your colours blend easily together, there are many ways in which they may be combined in the same area. If your joint colours are, say, Indigo and Pale Blue, then Indigo could go on the skirting boards and doors, and Pale Blue on the walls, curtains and cushions. And suppose that your colours combine to make another attractive one: what would happen if you mixed Pink and Gold, or Pale Yellow and Pale Blue? You might get a colour that you both like, in which case it would be a good background in a room where you want to spend a lot of time together. One couple, who were fortunate enough to have the space and the means for a large bathroom with a jacuzzi, made this room into a special kind of sanctuary, combining their favourite colours of Coral and Gold to form a deep terracotta for the walls, and then using the colours separately in the accessories: the towels, soap, candles and so on as well as the carpet and the main décor.

• • • • •

You have seen that every colour contains messages, some of which are welcome, and some of which are more challenging. The messages contained within your first colour choice are largely positive ones, reminding you of your hidden potential, reinforcing you in your purpose, and offering you the opportunity to see each other from a friendly place. There are always a few cautions as well as these gifts. In working with colour as a system, it is specifically the second colour choice that is regarded as the trouble-shooter; nevertheless, some of your challenges are also hinted at from the beginning. In general you need to recognise that, while the package of your inheritance contains your talents and your many good qualities, your life path also inevitably contains a number of lessons. The positive aspects of the colour are the qualities that you bring into life; and its more difficult aspects reflect some of those things which – at whatever unconscious or soul level – you have chosen, through which to develop and learn. So as you contemplate these initial colours, you may well find some guidance as to your path in life, and the types of situations which this might attract.

Suppose, for example, that you have chosen **Coral**: you are probably **sensitive** and **artistic**, you have a great sense of natural **beauty**, you are a **loyal** friend, and your generosity and your ability to **empathise** with others are wonderful strengths. With all these beautiful qualities, you may wonder why it is that you have attracted one situation after another in which you have felt **abused, hurt** and **under-valued.** Your life has probably presented you with plenty of these opportunities, so that you can learn to cultivate a proper sense of your own value, which depends on an assessment from your own inner wisdom rather than on the opinions of those around you.

So this aspect of your first colour choice gives you some food for thought as to why you were attracted to your partner. It brings you back to the question of polarity discussed in Part One, and provokes you to look at the ways in which your choice of each other as a partner challenges you, on the one hand, to expand your limits; or to see yourself, on the other hand, mirrored in your partner and to look yourself in the eye. Many people, for example, in the apparent innocence of what is often a victim state, are unwittingly asking their partner to tread – at least from time to time – all over them, so that eventually they learn to know their own value and strength. If your colours are very similar, this may well suggest that there is a good fundamental compatibility; but part of the initial attraction was almost certainly a process of mirroring which would eventually bring you up against some of the long-established habits that you yourself may need to kick. Suppose, for example, you have both chosen **Gold**, you are likely to share a **stimulating** and **active** partnership, with both of you ever-curious and **mentally alert.** You probably **laugh** a lot together; you are **sociable**; you are often gifted, too, with the capacity to connect with the kind of deep **insights**, and even **wisdom**, which might make you good **teachers** as well as **students**. But when you find yourselves competing for the attention of others, or both getting drawn into a downward spiral of **nervous anxiety** where you appear to feed one another's **tension**, it is helpful to withdraw and take a look at yourself and what your partner is mirroring back to you before you become locked into a worry syndrome or a power struggle.

Look at your own colour and at some of its more challenging aspects, and then ask yourself which of those difficulties come up to the surface in the interactions with your mate or loved one. What might you need to learn from this? Do you need to find a little more independence, detachment, faith, trust, compassion? Then, see if he or she will do the same. In this way, you can see one another as guides to help each other along the path which, even though it may sometimes feel a little thorny, is the one that will provoke you to realise most fully those gifts that you were born with.

BOUNDARIES

One last aspect of this first colour may also apply to some of the subsequent colours selected. It deserves to be mentioned here, because the concept of boundaries it is so vitally helpful in all your relationships. You consist of your energetic body as well as your physical ones, remember; so if you get clear about this, you can protect both your individual boundaries and those that define the relationship itself. **This is not just an idea but an "energetic" reality.** Your energy circuits extend way beyond the physical skin; you are interacting energetically with those around you all the time. This means that you are exchanging energy with one another. At certain times, and in certain relationships, this process of exchange remains fairly evenly balanced. At other times it can move way out of equilibrium. As long as you remain unclear about your boundaries, there are several ways that things can go wrong.

- *You may give too much, allowing your resources to become depleted.*
- *You may fail to make your own boundaries clear to others, so that your personal space is taken for granted or abused, leaving you feeling invaded and over-whelmed.*
- *You may fail to notice or respect the boundaries of others, and so do the same to them.*

It is the lack of clarity about boundaries which underlies much hidden conflict within families and friendships. It may be Dad who has for years felt overwhelmed by the family's taking for granted his unlimited access as the provider; it may be the godmother who discovers that a hidden part of the agenda was free baby-sitting services; it may be, in an extreme case, the young husband abandoned by his wife, leaving him only the legacy of another man's child. However these manifest, whether you are more inclined to "push" or "pull", problems with boundaries invariably have their origin in your own *limiting beliefs* about yourself and about your capacity to obtain all the energy that you need from the universal source around you. As long as you think you are powerless to create the quality of life you wish for, then you will make sure that you are as impotent as you feel!

Look at your colour and think how it may relate to this issue. If you are towards the Red end of the spectrum, do you have a tendency to project your energy outwards, and maybe sometimes to encroach on the boundaries of others? If you are towards the Blues and Violets, which are energies more inclined to move inwards, do you easily take on the burdens and troubles of others, to your own detriment? Are you drawn towards very pale colours, which may indicate that you are washed out by giving your energy away too easily?

Once you have gained some insights into your own boundaries, then look at the importance of your acknowledging your boundaries as a couple: of honouring the friendship you have sufficiently to ensure that your commitment to each other is the ground from which all other activities spring, and that this ground is nurtured and cherished, given space and time and warmth, as well as protection from those outside forces that might otherwise erode it. In other words, get clear about the boundaries that you both agree on: how much time you expect, and need, to spend together; how readily and frequently you receive one another's visiting relatives; how you allocate or share the household chores; how you organise your finances.

· · · · ·

Remember that, while there are always challenges even in what you bring to the most loving relationships, the most helpful way to approach your first colour choice is to focus on the strengths and gifts that it highlights. The energies of light and colour have the capacity to enlighten you and to reinforce in you that which is most noble and pure. Don't hesitate to bring in these colours in any way that takes your fancy, so that you can more powerfully re-member the scattered parts of yourself and become most completely the person you always intended to be. **In other words, the greatest gift you can receive through the recognition of your colours is to remember who you are**. It is this clarity, in the end, that draws towards you those people with whom you can live in harmony.

Now you are ready, when you feel like doing so, to move on and look at your second colour.

· · · · ·

An Optional Exercise

If you are interested in taking the examination of your colours a little further, now or later, this is an exercise for looking at your family tree. It can be helpful, when looking at the package of your genetic inheritance, or what you have brought into this life with you, to have a look at your ancestors, as well as at those relatives who are still alive.

Take a large sheet of paper and some coloured pencils, paints or whatever you like to use for drawing, and make a picture of your family tree with yourself at the centre. This may be drawn either as a simple diagram, as an actual tree, or in any other way that inspires you. Place your parents and both your sets of grandparents in whatever place feels appropriate. If these people are still alive, they may occupy a particular place within the main tree; if they have died you may visualise them as being above the tree in the sky, or below the tree in the earth. Use colours if you wish and find a place for any siblings you may have. Pay attention, too, to more distant family members, such as uncles and aunts: any of those people who have had some influence on you, even from far away.

When the drawing is complete, look individually at some of these influential members of your family – those you have found difficult as well as those you have related to easily – and write down as many of their good qualities as you can find. You may also write up to three (not more) of their more difficult qualities. Look again at your soul colour: look at its strengths, and also at its challenges, and notice the way that some of these characteristics are linked with those of your family and your ancestors. You cannot choose colours for another person, but you can use this tree to notice how the characteristics revealed by your own colours may coincide with other people close to you. Thank these people for all they have given you: the lessons as well as the more simple gifts.

When you have finished this exercise, don't throw this sketch away. It may be useful to return to it from time to time: on each return visit you may learn a little more about where you came from; this will give your more understanding about where you are, and where you are headed. If any family members are interested in joining with you in this exercise, it can be fun to incorporate their colour selection into the "tree" as well as your own.

Questions

In looking at your first choice of colour, and one another's, ask yourselves the following questions:

1 *What features do your colour choices have in common and in what ways do they differ?*
2 *How do the colours you have chosen in this first position indicate the ways in which you can offer each other support and a new level of understanding?*
3 *What do the colours suggest to you that you need to work on in order for each of you to gain a deeper understanding of where your partner is coming from?*
4 *Are you different in ways that complement each other comfortably, or does it feel sometimes as though you come from different planets?*
5 *Are your colours so similar that your communication always feels comfortable, easy and direct, or do you sometimes make the mistake of assuming that your partner intuits automatically how you feel without the need for explanation?*
6 *How do the colours you have each chosen in this position combine with each other, i.e. what new colour would emerge if they were mixed together? What does this combined colour tell you about your potential as a couple?*

chapter 10

THE POWER HOUSE

'Then you should say what you mean,'the March hare went on.
'I do', Alice hastily replied;' at least I mean what I say –
that's the same thing, you know.' 'Not the same thing a bit!'
said the Hatter. 'Why, you might just as well say that
"I see what I eat" is that same thing as "I eat what I see!"

Lewis Carroll

Alice's Adventures in Wonderland

D H Lawrence has been quoted as saying, or writing, that "*tolerance is a boring quality*". This is a good preparation for the next stage of a journey through colour, reminding you of the value in your life of a certain amount of friction. Nietzsche's statement that "*in heaven all the interesting people are missing*" (*Thus Spake Zarathustra*, Friedrich Nietzsche) expresses something of the same feeling. A world devoid of any sort of conflict or difference of opinion would be unspeakably dull. So would such a partnership or marriage.

In the early stages of an intimate partnership, the people concerned tend to be focussed on themselves and on one another. As time goes on and the friendship develops, the focus becomes wider as the partners begin to look outwards and the relationship finds its feet, as well as a place within a larger context. This stage is exciting and interesting, as the expansion and deepening of a couple's knowledge of each other provides the base from which they can explore new territory together, as well as further their own discoveries and growth.

Your first colour choice has addressed some of the aspects of the birth of your relationship. Will you now put aside your first colour spectrum card and refer to the second one you chose? The more certain you are that this is your very favourite out of the colours that remain, the more useful will be the insights you can gain from it. In looking at your second choice, you can contemplate the next phase of a relationship, which we can call the phase of adolescence and growth.

ADOLESCENCE AND GROWTH

Growth and adolescence are exciting, interesting, and also challenging in many ways. Growing pains hurt; and the mental and emotional challenges facing teenagers are notoriously difficult. So, this phase in the growing relationship between intimate partners also presents difficulties! Toddlers and adolescents are the most demanding of people to be around. As you begin to feel safer in the intimacy of a close partnership, the toddler and the adolescent within you will rise to the surface. When the physical body is attempting to release toxins and so heal itself, it produces a variety of symptoms, from headaches to skin rashes to fever and delirium. Part of the purpose of intimate relationship is to enable us to heal the wounds of our childhood. The emotional body behaves in a not dissimilar way to the physical one: in attempting to rid itself of early, deep wounds, it produces symptoms as various as mild irritation or depression through to temper tantrums or worse. You probably do not enjoy these symptoms, either in yourself or in those you live with. But they are inevitable if you are to grow, which involves leaving behind dead wood and making space for new shoots. There is an anonymous saying, in contrast to that of Nietzsche, that: *"Everyone wants to go to heaven, but no-one wants to die."* The second colour hints at some of the things that need to die in order for any of us to get a step nearer to heaven… In this "adolescent" stage of a relationship, then, it is more common than not to experience a degree of friction. But this chapter is called *"The Power House"* because friction, as you know from your physics lessons at school, *produces energy!* Energy itself is neither good nor bad. It is neutral: how you use it is up to you.

FRICTION

The friction that often occurs between and within people at this stage can be broadly categorised under two possibilities. Either:

1 *The people concerned find themselves sparking off against each other, producing* **outer** *friction,* **or:**

2 *One or other of the partners suppresses their thoughts and feelings, producing* **inner** *friction.*

Both possibilities produce discomfort for all concerned. The first one, outer friction, generally hurts both parties in a way that is immediate. As the first flush of romantic love settles into something of a routine, and the security of this brings your wounds to the surface, a couple will often start to rub up against each other. Whether the rubbing is slight or very marked, this produces some sort of friction which may be a mere tickle or may feel disastrous. Your immediate reaction to this may be panic and alarm. Perhaps you had hoped that you had found the perfect partnership: one which would proceed along the happily-ever-after lines so temptingly offered in the fairy tales. Forever beautiful and safe. **But intimate relationship is not about safety**. Intimate relationship, in fact, is likely to make you feel – more deeply than before – your vulnerability, as your *true colours* inevitably rise to the surface and expose your wounds. It is only later, as the work that two people are willing to do establishes a foundation of deep trust between you, that an intimate relationship can expand to give you a greater sense both of freedom and security than you have known in the past.

The truth is that the blandness of perpetual agreement would very soon leave most people feeling bored. Our mutual respect stems, at least in part, from the challenge of discovering and acknowledging another person's point of view. Without the necessary understanding of your partner, however, or the skills to communicate anything of that understanding, the friction produced between you is likely to cause only pain. The skill is to harness the energy produced by whatever friction there is, and to use it creatively. The energy, once it is understood and rightly used, empowers each person within the relationship and may be used to strengthen the relationship itself. The important thing to remember is that energy gives rise to *movement*, and where there is movement there is life, with all the possibilities that this brings for growth and change. It encourages you to become more aware of many aspects of yourself: your thoughts and feelings, your needs and desires, your weaknesses and strengths. This movement brings about the constant evolution that is every bit as necessary in your adult life as it was during the tricky process of moving through childhood and adolescence into the beginnings of maturity. Friction – inner and outer – is something that we have all experienced. But without any tools to harness it and use it creatively, it can get out of hand. Here is an example of such a situation:

Rory and Kit

It was Kit who, on the advice of a friend, requested a joint session for herself and her husband Rory. When asked which of them would like to talk first about what they were experiencing at present, they both began speaking at once.

> "It's Rory", said Kit, "he goes out with his buddies every night and never bothers with the children."

> "Kit's Mum is round the whole time", said Rory. "I never get a moment's peace."

After this the two of them struck up a heated argument:

> **Kit:** "I don't know how you afford all that Scotch. It's no wonder the children never get the clothes they need."

> **Rory:** "You're a fine one to talk. Your cigarettes burn a hole right through the top of our credit limit."

> **Kit:** "If you pulled your weight at home, maybe I wouldn't need to smoke."

> **Rory:** "A mother like yours would drive any man from home. I never knew I was marrying two of you."

And so on, except that this was a counselling session; so that the counsellor soon took control of the situation and brought some necessary structure into the encounter. The simple message was clear: the two people concerned were producing unlimited amounts of outer friction, which was achieving nothing except to accentuate each other's aggravation. Aggression was bouncing to and fro between them like a tennis ball, each shot returned with more impact than the one before. By the end of one session, it was clear that both were exhausted. It is always the responsibility of the people involved to decide whether they wish to solve a problem or to give up: this situation might well have been resolved had the parties been willing to do the necessary work. They did not return for a second session; for all I know, they are still waging war.......

This is one example of outer friction. The second possibility is that you may turn this friction inward, causing inner pain and wasting massive amounts of energy in the effort of suppression. The process of keeping our thoughts and feelings buried requires an inordinate amount of energy.

The consequence of such suppression is that a person functions on a *fraction of their potential energy levels*, because most of their energy is going into keeping the lid on the pressure cooker, in order to prevent the real person inside from jumping out of the pot! Moreover, the inner friction that is caused by this process

> *The process of keeping our thoughts and feelings buried requires an inordinate amount of energy.*

generally leads, in the long run, to the person who is doing the suppressing becoming unwell, in one way or another – mentally, emotionally or physically. Here is an example of the kind of thing that happens in an extreme case of inner friction:

Caroline

One client, Bill, who came for colour counselling alone because he was the only one of the pair who was ready to look at the issues involved, described the pattern which had continued in a marriage of some fifteen years' standing. His wife Caroline had suffered a drinking problem for most of that time, and this was becoming steadily worse. She also suffered from depression and chronic fatigue syndrome, usually failing to perform even the basic tasks involved in running a household. He described how, once a week or so, Caroline, as an evening's drinking progressed, became increasingly volatile and violent in her use of language. The rage would pour out, generally in Bill's direction because other family members did their best to remain out of the line of fire, until Caroline fell into an exhausted sleep. The next day, once she had recovered from the hangover, she invariably perked up considerably; she vigorously cleaned the kitchen, or found some other outlet for her hugely increased level of energy, which lasted for a day or two before the cycle started again. What was happening was that Caroline generally used all the energy she had in suppressing the whole package which was herself: her thoughts, her feelings, what she saw as all her failures and weaknesses; and co-incidentally, all her talents and strengths and gifts.

Every time she became drunk and lost control of herself, she effectively took the lid off the "pressure cooker". This made her feel a great deal better, until the pressure started to build up again. It was hardly surprising that she suffered from chronic exhaustion.

· · · · ·

When you recognise friction as an energy that you can use positively, you can let go of the pain and discover something new. You do this when you see each other and listen to each other actively, offering one another mutual empowerment. Instead of becoming caught up in a power struggle which comes from the fear in both partners that their needs will not be met, you can offer each other power consciously, and then all sides stand to win.

TROUBLESHOOTING

When you analyse the second colour you have chosen, you are, in a sense, looking for problems. You can think of this as troubleshooting: finding out what the difficulty is before that difficulty gets out of hand and runs riot. The colour chosen in this position offers a picture of what two people involved in a relationship *need* in order to grow towards the potential, within themselves and within the relationship, which was shown by the first colour chosen by each individual *and* by the combination of the colours chosen by both partners. Experience has shown that while a person's first colour choice reveals much about their essential quality, it is the second colour choice that draws particular attention to their *needs*. This empirical truth is partially explained by the fact that the second colour shows you, as individuals, what it is in the past that has given you the greatest difficulties, because – and this is the key: the second colour also reminds you of the potential for these very difficulties to become the source of your most potent gifts.

The second colour also reminds you of the potential for these very difficulties to become the source of your most potent gifts.

The person who has suffered the deepest fear over the speaking of her own truth may discover, once she has accessed the source of her crippling self-doubt, the passion and the conviction which transform her into a great teacher.

The child who has suffered the pain of a cruel mother may grow to become the wisest and most compassionate parent. The colour selected in this position alerts you to some of your most pressing issues and helps you to deal with them, as the conscious bringing of that colour into your aura (and your life) gently brings about a re-adjustment in that area of your awareness.

It is exactly those issues which present you with the maximum discomfort that are actually rendering you a service. Like all the pains you experience, they serve to draw your attention to those aspects in yourself where the energy flow is *blocked*. Blockage on any level interrupts your communication: when you dissolve

> *It is exactly those issues which present you with the maximum discomfort that are actually rendering you a service.*

these blocks, you find a *deeper level of communication with yourself* and thus a new degree of wholeness. This is what healing, or "wholeing", is about. This principle applies as surely to your relationships as it does to your physical body or your emotions. Areas of pain and distress are opportunities that alert you to the ways in which your communication with one another is impeded. Once you understand how the flow has become interrupted, you can explore the blockage and clear it out, freeing that channel. Your communication then becomes clearer and *more real than it was before you ever found yourself up against the blockage*. And it is real, clear communication that provides the nurturing ground for intimacy.

The skill of using the friction between us creatively has a lot to do with our responsibility in conveying to one another truths that are challenging in a way which the loved one is able to hear and accept. When you look at your own second choice of colour, you can be as gentle or as brutal with *yourself* as you wish. If you are working to achieve better communication with your partner, however, it is wiser to approach this colour with a little more caution. The *meaning* of your communication, in fact, (as the Hatter told Alice) is not necessarily what *you intend* by it but what the person with whom you are trying to communicate *receives* from it: these two things may well be different, unless you pay close attention to the quality of your message. Your second colour choice can not only bring a lot of clarification to the perplexing symptoms you suffer: it also provides you with a useful tool whereby you are helped to approach difficult communications with one another – and perhaps with yourself – in a constructive way.

It helps, therefore, to begin looking at your own and your partner's colours by making a checklist, like you did for your first colour, of the *positive* qualities that this second colour shows. This enables you to affirm yourself and your partner, to establish a harmonious and positive base from which you can begin to explore some of the difficulties: it enables you to turn around the energy produced by the friction between you and put it to good use. This is just as necessary when communicating with rebellious teenagers or with a business colleague. Before you read on any further, stop and make this checklist, and if possible use it to affirm those qualities in one another (or, if you are working alone, in yourself) that you appreciate and enjoy — even though there may be some among those qualities that have not yet fully shown themselves, because of difficulties that are getting in the way.

Here is an example of a couple who were able to do this:

Jo and Samantha

Jo and Samantha had met in hospital: Jo as an accident victim and Samantha as his nurse. Samantha nursed him for some weeks, and a friendship grew between them. Jo's injuries had been severe, and had included his face and head as well as his pelvis; so his physical recovery was gradual and, emotionally, it was hard for him to cope with both his reduced mobility and his altered looks, apart from the effect of the accident on his work. Nevertheless, it was his courage that had impressed Samantha from the start, as well as his perpetual sense of humour, and for a year she spent most of her spare time with Jo.

It took Jo nearly a year to complete his recovery. At this point, they began to expand their life together, meeting each other's friends; but instead of the enjoyment that Samantha had looked forward to, Jo became moody and hostile. Samantha had never known him behave like this; she had become used to a stream of bubbly affection and jokes. When Samantha tried to get Jo to talk to her, he refused. As Jo's depressiveness and hostility continued, the tensions built up and Samantha began to feel very angry. Bewildered and hurt, she could not understand the change in Jo's behaviour towards her. His strength, humour and affection seemed to have evaporated, leaving someone who was irritable and uncommunicative. At the same time, Samantha's usual gentleness and patience seemed to have given way to resentment and bouts of anger.

It was at this point that they came for colour counselling. They discovered that their fundamental preference for **Indigo** was exactly the same, giving them confirmation of what they had first recognised in each other. But where Samantha chose **Turquoise** in second place, Jo surprised himself by choosing **Orange**. Part of what this indicated was that although Jo had made a remarkable recovery, he was still in **shock**. Before the accident, he had enjoyed years of **independence** and had poured his energy single-mindedly into his work, requiring company only from time to time. He had never really been in love before, and the deep love he had developed for Samantha had come hand-in-hand with his inevitable **dependency** upon her. He had never been a man to do anything by halves; but now, finding himself without the physical strength for the enormous bouts of creative activity of the past, he had for nearly a year focussed the full intensity of his emotional energy on Samantha. During this time, she had insulated him from some of the effects of the trauma he had sustained. The new period of social interaction had acted as an unwelcome catalyst in the process of Jo's coming to terms with a massive life change.

Furthermore, it was bringing him into touch with more deeply buried pain: Jo's mother, extrovert and dynamic, had given most of her time in his childhood to the pursuit of the kind of friendship and activity outside the home which kept any deep emotional connection at bay. She had left Jo to fend largely for himself. The independent persona he had cultivated had served him well on a number of levels; but it had also kept him out of touch with the deeper aspects of himself and prevented him from finding intimate involvement with others. It was only now in seeing Samantha – young, happy and serene – in the company of other people who appeared so whole and carefree that Jo had come right up against the force of his shock, and of this more ancient pain. He was faced suddenly with realising what it was that he had to deal with: the loss of so much that he had been in the past, and a new level of encounter with his real needs. Nor could he believe that Samantha, young and attractive as she was, would want to stay for long with what he described as "damaged goods". Overcome suddenly by his own anxiety and grief, he jumped rapidly to the conclusion that Samantha would not want to continue to support him in his new state. Terrified, now, of losing her as well as what he saw as a large part of himself, Jo was also very shocked to realise how much he had come to need her.

The truth was that it was only Jo who was distressed by his physical state: Samantha's experience had been one of gratitude and relief that such a recovery in him had brought her the man she loved. Samantha, abandoned at the age of five by her father, had an unconscious expectation of loss: when Jo became so moody, this had come as confirmation of her deepest fears, immediately bringing to the surface the sadness that she had suppressed for much of her life. Samantha had had several boyfriends before she met Jo: friendships which had each tended to last a year or two. The common thread in these had been a feeling that she was neither heard nor seen. The colours she chose showed Samantha's need to be involved with people in a caring and committed way; she also needed to be recognised for who she was. Soon after she had met Jo and he began to regain consciousness, something in him had struck a chord deep inside her. Samantha very willingly looked at Jo's **Orange** in the second position, and thanked him for the **joyful** energy he had brought her even through his pain. She also acknowledged the intensely energetic quality in him that had fuelled some of their activities during the time they had already spent together, such as teaching Samantha to play the piano.

The **Indigo** and **Turquoise** colours Samantha had chosen confirmed her **peaceful**, **calm** quality, showing her as a person to whom others, drawn by an unusual quality in her of apparent stillness, easily turn. They also showed her deeper need for **security** which had largely gone unnoticed: her **loneliness**, and the feeling she had that in order to earn love she must work for it. In looking into the **Turquoise** that she had chosen in second place, Jo was quick to acknowledge Samantha's **generous** nature, the **creative** energy in her that expressed itself in every detail of her life including her approach to her work, and her **open-heartedness** which made her such a warm companion.

In the light of one another's acknowledged gifts, they then looked at the problem. Jo had felt so threatened by the feelings that had surfaced, as he had first come back into the outside world with Samantha, that he had been ready to believe that their life together was about to crumble. Seeing only Samantha's youth and strength, he had not appreciated her needs. Nor had he recognised the extent of his own trauma, or the very deep and irrational fear that had made him so dependent. Samantha, whose internal "tape" told her that no man she really needed would ultimately stay the course with her, had become caught up in sadness and fear. She could not find a way to break the deadlock, and together they had been ready to turn their worst fears into reality. The very thing which had originally brought these two together very nearly became the stake that divided them, until they both came to see that it was only their own fears which each was projecting on to the other. Once Jo understood that Samantha's need for him was as great as his was for her, he could begin to see her more clearly than before. Once Samantha understood that Jo had not, after all, lost interest in her – rather the very reverse – she could find the courage to reveal more of herself to him and move beyond her role as his nurse. It was not long before Jo's strength recovered enough for him to resume his work as an artist, and they soon came to see the crisis they had encountered as the beginning of a deeper and more evenly balanced relationship that blossomed and flourished.

• • • • •

The second colour choice indicates what types of issues you have found particularly burdensome as individuals. As it is yourself that you bring to every relationship you enter, it is inevitable that you will bring with you into your partnerships *whatever difficulties remain unresolved*, or in other words whatever "baggage" you are carrying around with you. The colours in this position help you to open the baggage containers and see what is inside. At this stage, it is helpful to look at your second colour and to write a second checklist: this time you should write down the more difficult qualities suggested by the colour you have chosen. This enables you to do two things: firstly, you can see more clearly some of your own underlying issues that have prevented you from coming fully into the potential that was at least partly indicated by your first choice of colour. Secondly, it enables you to look with more understanding, and therefore compassion, at these aspects in your partner. The "baggage" that is revealed by the second colour can then be seen more clearly if we look at it under several headings.

LOYALTY TO THE PAST

The legacy of conditioning and expectations from the *past* generally has greater power to exacerbate our difficulties in the present than what may actually be happening within the relationship *now*. The colours in the second position help to indicate those areas in yourself which have stood in the way of your finding and

What you bring into current relationships includes the conditioning of your past, which filters your perception.

living your potential, and therefore of enjoying the relationship, to the full. What you bring into current relationships includes the conditioning of your past, which filters your perception.

A good part of this, of course, comes from childhood experience: difficulties with the father, mother, or both; fear, arrogance, dependency and all sorts of other unresolved "hang-ups". This may include issues such as abuse, the supremacy of duty over love, religious beliefs, or a whole lot of other influences which have made it difficult for you to access your individual power and truth.

The net result of this conditioning is that people often find themselves trapped within the past. In this state of emotional imprisonment, as it is difficult to bring one's awareness fully into the present situation, it is very difficult either to grow or to *commit oneself fully* to one's partner. Here are a few possible scenarios:

- *Suppose the problem has been abuse: the victim of it finds that this has been the only example given to him of love, and this blocks him from either receiving or giving love in the present in a healthy way.*
- *Suppose that duty has been presented to the child as the abiding principle of her life: she is likely to grow up with the knowledge that she must work tirelessly to earn all that she needs, including love. This prevents her from feeding her present relationship with any kind of relaxation, fun or even spontaneous expressions of affection.*
- *Another possibility is a child who has been raised on a strict diet of religious dogma: he might be left with an inheritance either of superiority and self-righteousness, or fear, or a set of rules which leave him empty. This makes it difficult for him to accept the validity of another person's point of view and so hinders real communication; it also blocks off the path which would lead to the exploration of his own direction and truth.*

All these legacies from the past are likely to have a crippling effect on the quality of your current relationships, until they are recognised and understood. Their effect may to render you – usually unconsciously – more loyal to your parents and early teachers than perhaps you are to yourself and to your current central relationship.

You may find yourself caught up not only in over-loyalty to your deep past. This kind of problem often arises, when a person has left one close relationship and entered another. You may find you have carried through the unresolved issues from one relationship into the next, which can be very disappointing if you think you have just escaped from a load of problems you will never have to face again. This problem is different from the deep, unconscious patterns of loyalty that can keep you a prisoner of your early conditioning; but it is nevertheless a phenomenon that frequently arises and causes difficulties. It is by bringing through with you these unresolved negative expectations and patterns of behaviour from the past that you may come to find yourself involved in cycles of relationship which your conscious mind rejects because they continue to cause you pain.

How do you feel about the difficulties suggested by your second choice of colour? Is there anything in it that might alert you to ways in which your full participation in the present is limited by loyalty to conditioned patterns of thought? If your choice is **Blue**, you may find it helpful to look at the patterns of **authority** that surrounded your growing years. If it is **Olive Green**, has there been an atmosphere of **bitterness** or **hardship** that has moulded your expectations of what life will offer? If it is **Pink**, were you taught that it was "wrong to be selfish", so that you never learned to respect **your own needs** and now find that you have little to give and/or that you cannot freely receive?

FANTASY

This is another possible thorn that can be brought to the surface by your second colour choice. Fantasy, predominantly packaged as the **ideal** of romantic love (which is very different from the reality of it), is very alluring, and universally sought. This is self-evident from so much that we see around us: television, magazines, lonely hearts columns, romance novels, films, advertisements. We don't know very much about this ideal of cosy perfection, but we call it romantic love and, maybe, assume that it is something which will arrive on a plate when our number comes up. Sex and fantasy are inextricably intertwined, of course; and the advertisers' field day has run into some decades as our hunger for the everlasting perfect moment has provoked us to empty our purses for anything from ice cream to face lifts, lipstick to holidays in paradise.

This kind of fantasy, which is harnessed so profitably for commercial gain, is based on **illusion**: the belief that the pursuit of pleasure will somehow or other transport you from the world of hard experience and preserve you from suffering. The net aim of all the media channels that employ it is much the same: to create in you an insatiable appetite for fantasy in any form, and remove you from the real world in which you live. And this is the problem. You may get confused. You may lose touch with reality. Above all, you may lose any idea of how to work with what you actually have.

There is nothing inherently wrong with fantasy. It has played in important role in literature and the arts throughout history. The danger is for you to become so caught up in fantasy that it becomes your model for real life. Fantasy distracts you from your responsibility to own what you are and what you can create. Not only may you fail to see the *true colours* and, therefore, the real-life value of those with whom you are most intimately

> *The danger is for you to become so caught up in fantasy that it becomes your model for real life.*

involved: you may fail, too, properly to recognise your own. When you engage in fantasy, the danger is for you to look outside yourself for security, contentment and love: this causes you to lose touch with your own core, which is your centre of gravity, and this in turn throws you right off your internal balance. Fantasy in the wrong place means that nobody wins: you relinquish your power to create the real, two-feet-on-the-ground, living intimacy which evolves when two people look honestly at themselves and at each other and take responsibility for what they are and what they share.

In other words, you pass up the opportunity to bring genuine, living romance into your life. Not only might you be disappointed when your real-life partner falls short of the role models of your fantasies: you may also feel yourself to be a failure, because your own shortcomings may appear to leave you hopelessly out of the running when measured against these same figures of fiction. In order to stay with the fantasy and stave off the discomfort of reality, in order to avoid facing what you sometimes perceive as the pain of looking at yourself as you are, you may stuff down the alarm bells of your real emotions with alcohol, tobacco, drugs, sugar, ice cream, sex or any other temporary anaesthetic you can lay your hands on. If this trend once gets established, of course, it will carry over into your relationships.

Anita and Sam

Anita and Sam, the couple we have met from time to time throughout the text, chose **Turquoise** and **Gold** respectively in this second position. The Turquoise raised some questions about Anita's image of herself, which was at least partially rooted in fantasy: she saw herself as **gifted** and "**arty**", with the right to be eternally free. She needed to look at what she was actually achieving, and also at what a commitment to someone else involved. Sam's fantasy was different from Anita's: he had a slightly stereotyped image of himself as the "**successful**" provider, who would come home to a wife who would always be there to please him and praise him. **His ego**, and her **dreams**, needed knocking into reality in order for them truly to meet again as individuals.

What does your second colour tell you about some of your own fantasies that still lurk beneath the surface? Do you – for example – have a **Coral** tendency, hoping for the kind of ideal partner who will **shelter** you from your need to take responsibility? Does **Red** or **Orange** suggest a hidden belief that enough sex offers the passport to eternal happiness? Does **Green** or **Turquoise** show that you avoid any sort of commitment and **sit on the fence** in order to convince yourself that you are enjoying freedom? Or does **Gold** trick you into thinking that **glamour** brings fulfilment?

• • • • •

It is often the apparent safety of your fantasies that has stopped you from jumping over the edge into the frightening land of real experience. Yet, when you let go of fantasies about yourself and each other, you can cultivate the flesh-and-blood romance, and real intimacy, which is infinitely richer and more durable than anything available outside the relationships of your real life. When you pursue this route, you can root yourselves firmly in reality and create an environment that is safe enough for both of you to express yourselves, to grow and to develop your potential. Within this context of trust and mutual support, you can stop hiding your light under a bushel, and instead you can learn to shine that light and express the true colours of your thoughts, your feelings and your wishes. Each of you begins not only to feel safe enough to be completely yourself, but to allow one another to do the same thing. When you take the decision to jump over the edge, everyone stands to win.

PROJECTION

This is the process whereby, in an unconscious attempt to ignore our own weaknesses, we attribute these limitations to those around us. Sometimes you may experience the feeling of being angry or irritated with someone near to you, when in fact it may be a colleague or superior at work who is bringing up your own sense of powerlessness. When, as happens frequently, the projections are negative ones, their results can be quite destructive. The case of Samantha and Jo described earlier in this chapter is an example of a situation in which, for a time, two people projected their own fears on to their partner, with dire results. Part of what emerged as their colours were examined was that Jo had been projecting his unresolved anger and grief around his injuries on to Samantha who, before Jo's accusations, had not only felt neither anger nor grief but had also actively supported him through his own. His behaviour had then prompted Samantha in her turn to project on to Jo her childhood fear of abandonment; when Jo had never had any intention of leaving her.

Think about the times in your own life when you find yourself projecting your difficulties on to a close friend or loved one: the impatience, perhaps; the frustration, the over-concern with the ego, the control tactics that are in fact your own. When this happens it is a good idea to make a habit of stepping back, taking a few deep breaths and reminding yourself that these are your issues, rather than your friend's. Then you can look at your second choice of colour. If you examine your second colour in relation to this possibility, you can first acknowledge those difficulties that you recognise; and then remind yourself once more of the gifts that this colour can reinforce in you, once the issues have been dealt with.

Coming to know one another is the dynamic process of daring to expose yourselves within the context of an ever-deepening level of trust. It is, quite literally, the process of coming to know and respect your own and the other's true colours. This means that you can take responsibility for how you feel; you can stop blaming your friend or partner for feelings which, in actual fact, are your own. You can convey these experiences to that person, in non-threatening ways which they can hear and receive and which allow them in their turn to communicate to you what it is that they may themselves be feeling. This is a giant step towards the freedom that comes with taking responsibility for yourself.

MIRRORING

Another important aspect of the second colour choice is the phenomenon of mirroring, which we looked at briefly in Chapter 2. This is something that happens in all relationships all of the time and is not limited only to this stage. We mirror one another's gifts and also our faults. At the "adolescent" stage of a relationship in particular, however, this mirroring tends to present problems and must be understood, so that you can turn it around and see it as a useful tool. This is a good moment to reflect again on mirrors and the nature of light. Mirrors reflect the light, and colour is the expression of that light. But where there is light, there is also what Carl Jung originally described as the shadow, or our own darker side: these, too, are reflected in the colours you choose, and also by your partners and friends. Whether you are attracted to a person because of their apparent differences from you or because of their reassuring similarity, more often than not, you will find that, not far below the surface, there lies a hidden agenda: namely, those similarities to yourself that you had not spotted at first. The problem arises when these more hidden similarities relate, not so much to your beautiful qualities, as to those you would have preferred to ignore; or, in other words, when they apply to your shadow side. When you feel angry, irritated or upset by the behaviour of someone close to you, this may well be a useful symptom. Your irritation may be alerting you to some of your own less attractive habits: a propensity to criticise, perhaps; a failure to listen; a hint of cowardice?

Maureen and Dominic

Maureen and Dominic each brought children from their previous marriage into their relationship. Maureen's children lived with them; Dominic's visited for week-ends and holidays. Dominic had found it difficult being constantly around these new children and thought Maureen was much too soft with them; or, in other words, that she displayed weakness around them. Dominic also, from time to time, felt resentful over the amount of time and energy that Maureen gave to her children. When Dominic's children visited, Maureen felt exactly the same. Their **Pale Turquoise** and **Pale Green** in second place showed both of them their very similar **open-hearted** quality; but also their difficulty in claiming what they needed for themselves, which sometimes gave rise to an envy of others. The tendency to become **drained** by the demands of others was quite marked in both of them. They were soon able to recognise their similarities and use them to support each other, and their children, through this time of adjustment.

Similarly, you saw earlier that Anita and Sam found themselves confronted with some of their own qualities which had been hardest to accept: their stubbornness, their tendency each to assume that they were right, their unwillingness to sacrifice their own desires. All of these were qualities which, in fact, they shared.

It is particularly useful here to look at how your second colour relates to your partner's. If this is not possible, take the opportunity to look at the challenges that your colour suggests, and then ask yourself where and when you meet these same features in your friend or spouse. If this happens, how do you tend to respond? It is useful to remind yourself here that all colour comes from the same source, which is full-spectrum White light. The various colours can be seen as different facets of a diamond, all of which form a part of one entity. So it is with people: there are infinite details in which we differ from one another; but at a deeper level, we are very much more similar than we realise. When you react vehemently to something that upsets or irritates you in someone close to you, it is helpful to look at this as a pointer towards some aspect of yourself that you find difficult to accept.

· · · · ·

These are some of the categories you can use to identify areas of difficulty within yourself and your relationships. Any or all of these underlying patterns are likely to play a part in those episodes when friction – outer or inner – makes you feel discomfort or pain within a relationship. In most people's experience, the patterns have been so deeply underlying that they have been hidden. Once your colours begin to show you what is happening, what it is that is causing this distress, you can stop *reacting* to the pain you feel and begin instead to *respond*. Reaction is an automatic, knee-jerk thing; response is conscious, and therefore more powerful.

The first thing to do is to take a few deep breaths, instead of saying the first thing that comes into your head, and then to look at what it is in *you* that is causing you to react in the way you do. Kit and Rory gave us an example of two people who were caught up in patterns of reaction: this caused a power struggle between them in which they both

When you blame another person for how you feel you are also giving away your power!

became drained. The second colour you choose can help you to see what are your own vulnerabilities, what are the issues you have found most difficult, and to begin to take responsibility for these. This in turn means that you can let go of blame, because: when you blame another person for how you feel you are also giving away your power! When you stop blaming, and instead take responsibility for how you feel and think, you regain the power that you probably began to lose early in childhood.

• • • • •

In colour counselling, the second colour is the crux of the matter. Having discovered some of these causes, what do you do about it? Part of the answer is to know that in becoming aware of the problem you have already come a long way towards finding a solution. Another part of the answer is to *use* the colour, as a remedy. Saturate yourself with this second colour in any way you like (see Part Four). You can use it quite intensively as a remedy because, when you work with this colour, you will become more and more aware of what it has to teach. This enables you to turn your experience around so that you find the gifts, the hidden opportunities within the various crises of your experience. Take this opportunity to contemplate the issues raised by the colours you have chosen and, if possible, to discuss what comes up with your partner. Recognise that, as you work to release the old difficulties, more and more of the strengths, which you first acknowledged as a potential within you or your partner, will show themselves.

It is likely, when you begin working with colour in a remedial way, that the colour chosen in the second place will change in subsequent selections. Eventually, the choice settles down. In the meantime, beware of being too ambitious if you are thinking of re-decorating the house…. Three months hence, while your first colour stands a fairly good chance of remaining stable, your second one may no longer feel relevant. You will be ready by then, if you feel like doing so, to look at another set of issues, so as to bring further clarity and help you even nearer to the potential that your first colour has suggested to you.

The effort of sustaining an intimate and committed partnership born from romantic love can be daunting, especially after the first few hard knocks that generally form part of the journey into adulthood. But when you decide to accept the obstacles in your relationships as opportunities to get to know one another more deeply, you will create a space for yourself and for each other in which you are free to be completely yourselves. This must be the greatest gift that one human being can offer to another. You can find new dimensions within your partnership: a depth and breadth which you have not known before.

Through working to find truthful communication, you may have progressed a long way from the emotional climate of even some of your most recent ancestors. You can build a relationship whose foundation comes not from an external set of rules, but from something ultimately stronger and deeper: the inner security born of intimacy and mutual trust. It is this trust that provides the safe environment within which you can discover who you are and reveal yourself to your partner. This offers you an immense freedom.

Questions

1 *How have the processes of adolescence and growth manifested within your relationship? In what ways do you recognise that your partner has challenged you to stretch yourself and expand? In what ways has your partner helped you to recognise your weaknesses as well as your strengths?*

2 *When there is friction between you and your partner, does it express itself as fireworks or inner rumbles? In other words does it express itself as outer friction, or as the sort of tension that is pushed down into a box? What particular problems are you already aware of in your interactions with the most important person or people in your life?*

3 *In what ways have your loyalties remained tied to the conditioning of your childhood and your past? Are you aware of doctrines or beliefs that keep you bound to the influences of your past, and prevent you from being fully open to listening to your partner or friend?*

4 *Are you aware of any negative habits or expectations that you have brought with you from a previous close relationship into your current one?*

5 *What part does fantasy play in your life? Is it just a pleasant distraction from time to time, or does it dominate and undermine your real experience?*

6 *In what circumstances are you liable to project your moods or expectations on to your partner, blaming him or her for how you feel?*

7 *In what ways do you and your partner or family members mirror one another? What kinds of difficulties does this cause?*

TRAVELLING HOPEFULLY

The highest reward for a person's toil is not what they get for it,
but what they become by it.

John Ruskin

I f you want to go further in your journey through colour, and bring back into your life the power to make of it the rich, fulfilling experience that you deserve and need, you may now go on to examine the third colour you have chosen, and finally, the fourth.

With the bulk of the troubleshooting behind you in the scrutinising of your second colour choice, you can now relax and be prepared to look at your third colour - for the main part - from a positive stance; and you can then look forward to a completely optimistic view of your fourth and final choice.

In Aura-Soma colour counselling, your third choice of colour reflects the significant aspects of what is going on in the present, while your final choice suggests the direction in which your past and present thoughts and actions are leading you. This perspective also applies here: however new or however long-established your relationship may be, your third colour reflects aspects of your journey which are significant at the present time. It can act as a reminder to live in each moment rather than get hung up in the past or the future. As Deepak Chopra tells us: *"The past is history, the future is a mystery, and this moment is a gift. That is why this moment is called 'the present'."* (The Seven Spiritual Laws of Success, Deepak Chopra, Bantam Press.)

In the context of relationship, there are several further implications to explore as you look at the third colour you have chosen.

EARLY ADULTHOOD

The third "season" in a relationship can be seen as the time of early adulthood, and your third colour choice corresponds in some sense to this stage. At an earlier period in our lives – in childhood and to some extent in adolescence – there is a tendency in most people to assume that adulthood will automatically confer on us the ability to cope with all contingencies. Unless children are surrounded by actively warring adults, they will often imagine that grown-ups, unlike children, have overcome their need to quarrel. In practice, however, it is much more often the case that grown-ups, until they find the tools to understand their patterns, have become products of their own conditioning and have merely learned to suppress their true feelings, with some of the difficult consequences discussed in the previous chapter. Early adulthood is the time when, if you choose to do so, you can begin to gather up the skills and learning gained through the testing and often painful lessons of childhood and adolescence and turn them to positive use. But it is difficult, or even impossible, to do this without the necessary equipment.

The passage into adulthood can be defined as the journey towards a place where we learn to accept full responsibility for ourselves and what we create. The third colour helps you to look at this emerging "adult" stage of your life, and of your relationship, with a view towards whatever is positive in your connection. Your joint colours in this third position can be very useful in affirming whatever it is that each partner is bringing to the relationship at the present time. Taking responsibility for yourself implies that you have stopped giving away your autonomy and your power and are ready to approach close relationship from a stronger place, bringing to it the personal resources you have to share. This is why you can look at your third colour choice from a substantially positive perspective. Early adulthood implies that you are acquiring the power to direct the course of your life and thus to stay on the positive side of the colour you select.

By now, you have enough colours each to take stock of the general state of things. These colours can help you to understand the respects in which you have chosen each other because of your similarities, with the comforts and discomforts that this brings. And they show you the ways in which, through your differences, you also challenge one another to expand and learn.

THE CONSCIOUS GIVING OF POWER

The last chapter demonstrated some of the ways in which couples can become caught up in a struggle for power. A power struggle is always based on some kind of fear: the fear that our needs will not be met. As long as the struggle continues, both parties lose out, each becoming increasingly exhausted by the draining of energy that such a battle involves. You glimpsed, in the previous chapter, at an alternative: once you take responsibility for the way you feel and respond, you can turn the whole thing around, so that a *struggle* for power becomes the very opposite: a partnership in which each partner consciously *offers* power to – or *empowers* – the other. In this situation both parties win. You reap what you sow. Whatever you give out you get back, in one way or another.

If each partner determines to give power to the other one, through respect, through the active listening that such partnership involves, then each partner inevitably also receives an equal amount of energy back from his partner or friend. So, for example, if you say "You make me mad", you are giving *up* your responsibility and your power; through blame you are letting it slip away, unnoticed, to another person. You are giving away your energy, in other words, unconsciously. If, on the other hand, you say "I feel angry when you speak to me in that way; I would like to talk about it", this shows that you are taking responsibility for the way you feel, and it also gives an opportunity to the other person to express what he or she feels. This, instead of threatening the person you are talking to, opens the door towards a conversation, and a potentially constructive resolution.

ENJOYING THE DIFFERENCES

Once a couple begins to relate to each other from this place of self-responsibility, they can begin to enjoy the differences, instead of seeing them as a cause for distress. In the second, "adolescence and growth" stage of a relationship, you have seen that a couple tends to find that the differences between them cause difficulties. You have looked at how an understanding of these differences through colour can help a couple to turn these around to see what lies behind them, to gain a deeper level of mutual trust and support. Now, as you look at the third colour, you can begin not only to accept the differences between you, but to welcome them as the *very thing that keeps the relationship alive and growing*. The resolution of conflicts becomes a stimulating process in which each partner can value and honour the place that the other person is coming from, and recognise that this place is different from the one that they come from themselves.

It is, at least in part, these very contrasts between you that have caused you to be attracted to one another from the beginning. In coming to the other person, you have recognised, at whatever level, that this person has something that you lack. In a heterosexual relationship, there is the obvious distinction between man

> *The resolution of conflicts becomes a stimulating process in which each partner can value and honour the place that the other person is coming from.*

and woman; and even in most intimate relationships between people of the same sex, each of the pair will tend towards a different end of the male-female spectrum. As already discussed in Chapter 2, when you are seeking a partner, you are not only attracted to what feels familiar and comfortable, but you are also looking to the other person for what you lack and may feel that you need. In a healthy state, this is different from dependency and co-dependency, in which people are bound together in a way that is mutually more destructive than creative, through their individual sense of emptiness and their consequent need for another person either to look after them or to validate them.

Anita and Sam

Let us return briefly to the couple we have followed through the text. In third place Anita and Sam chose **Pale Violet** and **Coral** respectively. This choice showed two interesting things in particular:

1 *Both Anita and Sam remained distinctly individual and different from one another.*
2 *They had each moved nearer to their partner's "soul" or original choice. Sam's Coral is near to the Orange that Anita chose first; her Pale Violet has the same essence as Sam's original Violet.*

This discovery helped them to see how much closer they had come in the present to a mutual understanding of where they had both come from, and it also reinforced their separate gifts.

• • • • •

- *What colour have you chosen as your third one?*
- *If your partner has also chosen a third one, how do your colours relate to each other?*
- *What does it show about your different needs, your varying interests?*
- *What gifts do you value in your partner that you know that you lack? What talents or qualities do you have that your partner lacks? (These probably form a vital part of what attracted that person towards you in the first place.)*

Trust your choice; the colour may remind you of the benefit of reinforcing and cultivating the qualities in you that your partner enjoys.

THE SHARING OF RESOURCES

The third choice of colour may offer some suggestions in relation to the qualities and skills that each partner brings to the relationship. It is the sharing of personal resources and skills that each person brings which can provide the co-operative base on which their connection thrives. Any friendship survives on the basis of an exchange of energy, whatever form that energy takes. In every partnership, there has to be the emotional, mental and spiritual equivalent of a sound economic base, as well as a material one, if the relationship is to thrive. In simple terms, there has to be give and take. With the best will in the world, if a situation arises in which one or the other partner is giving much more than they are receiving, this will before long rebound on both partners in negative ways: the one who is doing all the giving will build up resentment in one form or another; and the one who is withholding their energy from the partnership will sooner or later begin to suffer a reduced sense of their own value and thus gradually lose their self-respect.

If one or other partner remains cramped by issues that are not yet dealt with, both of them will find it difficult to bring their energy fully into the present and, therefore, to contribute in full to the fair exchange of energy and resources that sustains the running of the relationship on a day-to-day basis. The consequence of this is that the relationship will be deprived of its essential food, which is the mutual exchange of energy, whether this energy is physical, emotional, mental or spiritual. Once these issues have been honestly faced, however, there is every opportunity for a couple to get in touch with their real talents and to bring these into the relationship as a mutual offering of gifts.

A relationship thrives where there is a mutual exchange of energy between people who are each coming to the other with the intention of pooling their resources. This is not to imply that this energy exchange must be solely a material or tangible one. One partner may provide material security, while the other offers emotional support; one person may bring greater experience and a level of teaching and guidance, where the other offers companionship, laughter and the readiness to discuss ideas. The nature of the gifts we bring is immaterial. What is important is simply that the relationship find a level of equilibrium through the intention and ability in each partner to realise their own talents and strengths and to bring these to one another to share.

Look at your third colour with this in mind.

- *Does this colour remind you of any qualities in yourself that you had buried or forgotten, and which will help you to contribute actively and dynamically to keep your relationship alive and thriving?*
- *What are the different areas in which each of you recognises that you are stronger than the other?*
- *Where are the areas where either of you welcomes the other one's support?*

HABITS AND LIMITING BELIEFS

The colour in the third position is almost entirely approached from a positive stance; but it can also be helpful sometimes in offering an indication of whether you as an individual are still trying to cope with some of the old problems and difficulties, or whether you have moved on. If a person chooses, say, **Indigo** and then **Pale Blue** and then **Blue** and then **Violet**, this suggests he is still having a hard time with the issues that have been difficult all the way along. This might mean that, in practice, the choice of **Blue** in this third position speaks more about the person's tendency towards **depression** than about his **peacefulness**; that it indicates more about his **difficulty with communication** than with his ability to accept full **responsibility** for himself; and so on. On the other hand, if something different from these two previous choice – **Yellow**, for example – comes up in third place, this suggests some dynamic movement. The person has most likely dealt with many of the difficult aspects of his Blue tendencies and is now enjoying an optimistic and sunny outlook, full of the Yellow joys of spring.

In the same way, this third choice can address this aspect of your relationship and give you a suggestion of how things are going at the present time. How far have you each come in fulfilling the combined potential that was shown by the interaction of the first colours you each chose? How well have you incorporated the lessons learned through the difficulties reflected by your second choice of colour? Have you overcome your **Red** tendency to lose your temper every time something upsets you? Have you begun to see that your **Gold** habit of wanting the centre stage is not actually helping you? Have you found ways of coping with your **Violet** tendency towards despondency?

The force of habit is very powerful and your individual colour choice here can help you to understand something of how your habits can imprison you, in order that you can learn to leave them behind and come fully into a greater freedom. Suppose that someone has chosen **Magenta** first, and then **Pink**. These colours suggest a whole lot of qualities, such as a great capacity for **love** and **generosity**; a sense of **commitment** and **purpose**; powerful **intuition**; and the willingness to **sacrifice** herself for a cause. They also indicate that this person sometimes has a tendency towards **escapism**; that she is often **needy** emotionally; that she has a **problem in taking a firm stand**; and, perhaps, that she is suffering from **anger** which may well be unexpressed. These difficulties are inevitably rebounding in some way within the dynamics of her relationship. If, therefore, in third place she is drawn to **Green**, this would suggest that she has worked through some of the difficulties that were shown by these colours, and that her focus is now in a new direction. If her partner, too, has moved forward to a different colour, it will be easy for the two of them to look at the interaction of their respective colours in third place in a light which is largely constructive.

A brief look here at the physiology behind your habits helps you to see the way in which these build up, and also shows you how useful colour can be in letting go of their hold on you. Neuro-science has brought great breakthroughs in our capacity to understand the powerful force exerted by habitual patterns of behaviour and thought. Every time you have a thought, or a feeling, or an experience, neurons (which are nerve cells designed to conduct impulses) send electro-chemical messages backwards and forwards across neural pathways; these messages are a bit like traffic moving around the brain. Billions of these are moving around the brain at the same time, allowing you simultaneously to be thinking, feeling and doing all kind of things. Whenever you do or feel or think something for the first time, you form a neural connection, a thin strand which then becomes thicker and stronger each time this action, or feeling, or thought is repeated. This is like strengthening a muscle through regular exercise. It means, of course, that it becomes easier and easier for this pattern to be repeated, until the pattern becomes more or less automatic.

When these habits are ones that bring happiness and fulfilment, all is well and good. This accounts at least partly for why it can be so powerful to use daily affirmations. The difficulty arises when the habit is one that *obstructs your happiness* or *hinders your growth*. The neural connection can take you over, so that you act like a passenger in a high-speed train. Then it gets pretty hard to get off the train. But these neural connections are not dissimilar to muscles, in that, when they are not used, they become smaller, and even eventually wither. So, when your choice of colour brings to your attention a way of being that is limiting you in whatever way, you have the power to alter it swiftly and radically if you choose to do so, by the conscious decision not to invest this particular neural connection with any more *energy*. Colour is a powerful ally in this process, because not only does it alert you to your more self-destructive habits, but it hands you the tool to overcome these habits quite painlessly. This Blue person, for instance, may well help herself greatly by plunging into a deep Blue-coloured bath, or saturating herself with this ray in any way she chooses, until her need for the colour is satiated. On the other hand, or later, considering the extent to which she has shown herself to be stuck in a Blue place, it may be helpful for her to look at its complementary opposite and to find ways of bringing this into her life. The very Blue person quite probably needs to bring in some Orange energy; the Yellow person, caught up in deep habits of fear, could do with some Violet; and so on.

It may be that the person heavily weighted in their colour choices towards one part of the spectrum has a dislike for certain other colours. If you experience this, it is likely to mean that the colour has some kind of unpleasant association for you; and so the short-term use of the rejected colour may well to help bring a difficult, sad or frightening memory up to consciousness, which can then be dealt with, so that you can move on. There is no need to splash the hated colour all over the walls of your living room; you can simply remember to bring a little more of it than usual into your diet, rub it onto your body, bathe in it, or use any of the methods suggested in Part Four and notice how things change.

Sam and Anita, at this stage, were still only just on speaking terms. Yet they were both open to looking for a solution. Each of them recognised how entrenched they were in some of their more difficult habits, and they set themselves the task of overcoming these. They both worked quite consciously with the issues raised, bringing the necessary colours into many different aspects of their daily routine. A few months later, when they felt ready for a new session, they both chose Turquoise in third place. This coincided with a time when they had found a new willingness to co-operate with each other; they were nevertheless surprised to see that they had both chosen exactly the same hue.

In general, the third choice of colour is an indicator of the ways that you work together, enjoy one another's friendship, and treat each other with honour and respect. This mutual understanding provides the ground for both partners to function at optimum levels.

CREATIVITY

With trust and true communication established, through the process of working through and understanding the issues raised by the colour in the second position, both parties in a relationship now have the resources to be well established in an atmosphere within which they can thrive. Against the background of mutual support provided to both by this atmosphere, they may well now be ready to create a space for the development of their creativity. Such creativity is a vital part of our humanity and is something which is frequently underestimated or misunderstood. Creativity, essentially, is the bringing of positive thought and energy to whatever we engage in: it is the positive thinking that builds rather than destroys. Its expression varies according to our talents. Every person brings certain qualities and gifts into life, and the urge to express these in some creative way is as basic as the drive to survive. To create for yourself and one another a space in which each of you can grow to become the most creative that you are able to be is to honour your commitment to each other at the deepest level.

> *To create for yourself and one another a space in which each of you can grow to become the most creative that you are able to be is to honour your commitment to each other at the deepest level.*

Your third colour choice gives you the opportunity to look at some of the ways in which your creative gifts may find expression. When two people encourage each other in this way, this also helps the relationship to expand and thrive. Creativity can mean almost as many things as there are people: for one person, it may be expressed through the raising of children; for another, through the creation of a garden or a home; for another, through dance; for another, the building of a corporation. No matter what form the creative activity takes, each partner can most profoundly love the other through the support they give to its cultivation.

RETAINING YOUR INDIVIDUALITY

The emphasis so far has tended towards the help that a couple can obtain through colour to discover a deeper togetherness by working through the differences that you bring to your union. As you look at this third phase, where you are contemplating some of the implications of adulthood, you can look at another aspect of a healthy partnership. The colour chosen in this third position acts as a reminder to each of you to honour both your own and each other's uniqueness and separateness. By honouring the integrity and completeness of each other as individuals, you maximise the possibility of each coming to the relationship from a place of abundance, where you can bring the fullness of what you share, rather than a demand for what you need or are hoping to receive. There is always a danger within intimate relationships of one or both partners losing their sense of individual identity and becoming lost or swamped within the all-enveloping sense of the two becoming one. The colours chosen in this third position help each of you to see something of your own individual development and your own strength.

Sandra and Bernard

Sandra and Bernard came to colour with the positive intention of avoiding the mistakes of their previous relationships. Bernard had been held at emotional gunpoint by a spouse who had frequently reminded him of the sanctity of marriage. Half an hour's delay in returning from work had brought a battery of questions to account for it. In this atmosphere of suffocation, the love between them, as well as Bernard's confidence and productivity in the outside world, had withered. In third place, in this comparatively new relationship, Bernard's **Coral** stood in total contrast to Sandra's deep **Indigo** and confirmed them both in their enjoyment of some very different thoughts and pursuits, and also in their mutual respect. Both of them, after their similar previous experiences, had developed some considerable respect for the sanctity of the individual. Thus, Bernard's **Coral** affirmed him and reminded Sandra of his need for sociable **companionship**; the **creativity** and **love of beauty** in him that required him to work in close **co-operation** with others. This was not what Sandra always wanted for herself; her **Indigo** was a reminder that there were often times when what she needed was **solitude** and the time to think quietly: it was this privacy that enabled her to be at her most creative. Unlike Bernard's previous partner, Sandra was quite happy for him to pursue his interests among his own friends, not all of whom were those with whom she would have chosen to spend her time: he would return contented and enriched. Bernard in his turn was happy to acknowledge Sandra's need for sometimes quite long periods as a kind of hermit, from where she would emerge refreshed and companionable.

MATURITY

To complete your colour *reading*, you may, if you wish to, choose a fourth, final colour, if you have not already done so. After birth, adolescence and early adulthood, this colour can be seen as relating to a later stage: the phase of maturity in a relationship.

Above all, the colour chosen in this final position combines with all the colours already chosen to complete a picture of something fundamental to every individual, as it is to humanity as a race:

- *Where you have come from,*
- *Where you are, and*
- *Where you are going.*

It is this fourth colour in particular that helps you to see the last of these three: where you are going. This is not to suggest that one single colour can offer a sweeping panorama that encompasses all that lies ahead; but rather, it recognises that the future exists in each new breath that you accept, in each new step that you take. You contribute actively to the quality of this future through everything that you have done, and been, in the past, and through all that you are and do in the

> *By the quality not only of your actions, but also of your thoughts and expectations, you create – step by step – the reality that becomes your life.*

present. By the quality not only of your actions, but also of your thoughts and expectations, you create – step by step – the reality that becomes your life.

The fourth colour, no matter how long two people have actually been together (or how old you are), may have something to say which reflects the possibilities for a more mature stage of your relationship: it represents the summation and the fruition of all that has gone before and that contributes to the future you are creating. Every couple has a history. Their history, however, is more than just a record or chronicle. It is the very stuff of their own unique story, a tapestry woven of all the threads that have entwined themselves to form the mini-epic of their shared life. For some, this may have been a story of trials and storms; for others, a journey of comparative ease; but for every couple that has stayed together over a certain length of time, then, even if that cycle is drawing to a close, there has been something of value.

It stands to reason, therefore, that you do best to interpret this final colour entirely from a positive standpoint. If you have only been together for a short time, there is still some value in selecting this fourth colour if you wish to. Suppose it is Gold that you have selected in this position: you can notice and appreciate the deepening sense of your own value; you can trust the power of your insight; you can enjoy the human company around you with the wisdom, warmth and humour that this enables you to share. And, if your partner finds himself drawn towards the Red in this fourth position, you may perceive the strengthening of his physical energy; his passion and determination to succeed in the projects he embraces, and perhaps feel grateful for his eternal enthusiasm. In addition to this, you can combine the two colours that you have both selected in fourth place and discover that, together, your chosen hues blend to Orange; a hue which suggests, in this position, that you have let go of the old dependent and co-dependent fears (a major difficulty in the Orange) and can now discover and co-create a state of union that is based on the sharing of laughter, joy and bliss.

Just as any effort of creativity – a painting; a piece of music; a book – is a process of finding something within yourself, so the creation of an intimate relationship is a journey towards the discovery of yourself as well as the real meeting of the one with the other. As you embark on this journey, you do not know what you are going to find. As you first learn to reveal yourselves and then empower each other through a deepening process of trust, and as you grow and develop as individuals within the mutual support you offer one another, then the journey becomes a deepening adventure. With the well-rooted sense of commitment that a couple has achieved by the time your relationship reaches maturity, each new day is a weaving of another thread in the creation of your shared tapestry.

It is best to view the final colour in the context of all that has gone before and in relation to all the other colours within your joint selection, knowing that the process of analysing the earlier chosen colours has thrown light on much in your connection that was previously mysterious, wonderful or painful. Nevertheless, in offering you a signpost to the direction in which you are headed, as well as showing you something of where you have come – both individually and together – in your journey, this final colour can offer considerable support to a couple who wish to delve deeper and to make sense of much that has gone before.

The fourth choice of colour that a couple makes in a consultation sometimes draws attention to circumstances or shared passions that unite people even after the most trying experiences. Or, it can affirm you in the attempts you are making to cultivate qualities such as compassion, generosity, imagination, or any others that presented difficulties in the past. The interpretation of this last colour in the selection, then, is more of an intuitive than an analytical or rational process. You can learn best by doing it: look at the colours you have both chosen, explore their significance, make lists of the qualities associated with them that most closely resonate with you; and discuss them.

Love is not merely a feeling, or an impulse. It is a complex journey that we make simultaneously on many levels: spiritual, mental, emotional and physical. It is a journey away from the dependency and co-dependency that has characterised the fear-based states of your earlier life and towards something new, richer and freer. This is the state of *interdependency* in which each of you recognises the other's value, honours their separateness, and creates the space in which both parties may grow towards the fullest expression of your unique creativity. Your ultimate destination in this journey is the place of unity that comes when you have discovered the understanding of yourself and of each other that will give rise to the most complete acceptance and compassion.

The instinctive grasp of the insights offered by the colours you have chosen does not grow overnight. Colour, being the universal energy of light which exists within the core of us all, is at once both simple and absolutely profound. To fill in and then study your own colour charts presented at the end of this chapter will offer you the opportunity to gain some of these insights at once. Then, if you stay open to what colour has to show you, more understandings will follow.

A question that is often asked is "will my/our colours change?" This question has already been at least partially answered: yes, they will. Life is a journey; it is never a finished product. The old Chinese proverb states that it is better to travel hopefully than to arrive: in other words, the important moment is the present one. The more you can let go of outcomes, the more fully you can partake, moment to moment, in the process which is the unfolding journey of your life.

How much the colours change over time is very much a personal matter. It is true that everyone has their own particular colour or colours; but it is also a fact that it can take one person a very long time to recognise these colours, where another person will be instantly drawn to the ray that is familiar to them and that continues to resonate with them for the rest of their life. The conditioning patterns acquired in childhood clothe our consciousness in clouds, or filters, which tend to obscure our view of that pure consciousness, the central aspect of ourselves. What happens is that, as we work with the energies of colour and light, this very process gradually removes these filters, so that, as time goes on, we see more clearly. For many people, the first choice will remain the same from the very beginning, while the second choice will take a little while to settle down and the third and fourth colours continue to change for some time. For some, even the first choice will continue to alter for a while. It is likely, however, that by the time you have reached this point in working with this book, you will already have discovered that your choices of colour reflect the truth as you understand it at the present moment. Truth is neither absolute nor static; like the cells of your body, it continually renews itself and grows with you as your understanding deepens.

Questions

1 *What does your third choice of colour tell you about your journey away from the problems of adolescence and towards adulthood? Did your second colour choice suggest difficulties which are shown to be (at least partly) resolved in the positive qualities suggested by this third colour?*

2 *How aware are you of the differences between yourself and those closest to you? Do these differences present themselves as a threat to your sense of safety and security, or do you welcome them as something to enjoy?*

3 *In what ways do you and your partner offer each other an exchange of resources? What do you like to offer that enriches the experience of your partner? What does your partner bring to you that you might otherwise lack?*

4 *What habits do you find very hard to kick? Are these habits causing you pain either in your individual life or within your relationship?*

5 *Do you have a strongly developed sense of yourself as a valuable individual? Does your partner have a similar sense of his/her worth? Or, do you depend overly on one another for your sense of identity and self-respect?*

6 *What kinds of creative activity do you enjoy? Are you, and your partner if you have one, consciously attempting to encourage one another in any kind of creative activity?*

PERSONAL SELECTION CHART

Partner One

NAME: _____

DATE: _____

Colour No. 1:
Gifts   Challenges

Colour No. 2:
Gifts   Challenges

Colour No. 3:
Gifts   Challenges

Colour No. 4:
Gifts

Comments:

PERSONAL SELECTION CHART

Partner Two

NAME: _____

DATE: _____

Colour No. 1:
Gifts   Challenges

Colour No. 2:
Gifts   Challenges

Colour No. 3:
Gifts   Challenges

Colour No. 4:
Gifts

Comments:

COMBINED SELECTION CHART

Partner One   ## Partner Two

Name _____   Name _____

Colour No. 1 = Plus Minus	Colour No. 1 = Plus Minus
Colour No. 2 = Plus Minus	Colour No. 2 = Plus Minus
Colour No. 3 = Plus Minus	Colour No. 2 = Plus Minus
Colour No. 4 = Plus	Colour No. 4 = Plus
Comments:	

PART FOUR

RAINBOW: A SIGNPOST TO THE FUTURE

Life can only be understood backwards,
but it must be lived forwards.

SOREN KIERKEGAARD 1813 – 1855

chapter 12

ACCESSING COLOUR

I conquered death, and arose; brought Immortality to light,
and painted on the walls of Time a Rainbow for the sons of men.
And what I did all men shall do.

The Aquarian Gospel of Jesus Christ

W hich colours, out of those chosen, are the most necessary for you? Part Two has shown you a good part of the answer to this. Here's a brief recap. The selection made in the first position is a reflection of your true quality. It is good to have a certain amount of this colour around and available; but generally not in too large quantities. In many cases, you will find that there is an intensity in the way you resonate with the first colour that you choose. On the walls of your house, for example, it is quite likely to feel like an overdose.

The first colour, in small quantities, acts as a constant reminder to you of who you are. It can also offer a frequent topping up of the ray that you need, because there is often a tendency to give of this ray too easily. However odd this may sound, it is a very familiar experience for those working therapeutically with colour. A Violet or Magenta person, for example, is likely to choose work that involves caring for others; which may mean that you are unconsciously dishing out Violet or Magenta energy to those you are caring for all day and that your own "supplies" of this vibration are getting depleted. Similarly, a teacher or a student is often a "Yellow" or "Gold" person, and may well, therefore, be using Yellow or Gold quite intensively and have need of replenishment. The more work you do on your boundary issues, the less depleted you will become. Meanwhile, it is helpful to keep yourself reinforced with the relevant colour energy.

However, as already suggested in Chapter 10, it is, above all, your second choice of colour that you need to introduce into your everyday routine. You can view this as a type of medicine that you need while working through a particular stage of your life. Your needs will change; and if you bring this second colour consciously into your life for a few weeks or months, you will find that the issues around that colour will begin to resolve themselves; at which point you will be ready to go on and look at some colours again and see how your choices have changed. The main purpose of both the third and the final choice of colours is to bring to light the current and future picture, as shown and discussed in Chapter 11. You will lose nothing, and will gain a certain amount, by bringing these colours into your home and into many other aspects of your life; but if you wish to put your attention towards one colour at a time, then it is the second colour, for each of you, that is the most important.

There is a whole range of ways in which you can bring colours consciously into use. You can wear them, of course. A burning desire to don Pink pyjamas or a bright Turquoise sweater makes more sense than it might once have done in the light of the colour information you now have available. There is also some reasonable evidence that to paint the appropriate hues onto your walls and to include them in your furnishings will have a significant effect. Indeed, the practice of using colour to affect our mood, health and consciousness goes back thousands of years. This knowledge is now being harnessed not only in prisons and hospitals, but also by enlightened management teams who are attempting, through the conscious use of colour in the workplace, to promote happiness and harmony in their workforce with the intention of maximising the company's efficiency (plus other amazing things, such as reducing the heating bills). All of this harks back to the methods used by Egyptian, Grecian, Indian and other healers some three thousand and more years ago. They even incorporated their use of colour into their architecture, designing their healing temples in such a way as to divide the light from the sun through a prism which directed the various rays into different rooms within the temple: the patient would then bask in the ray which was needed the most. Sunlight, and the colours that it contains within its spectrum, has been with us as our primary medicine since the dawn of time.

You can follow your own instinct in accessing colour in any of the ways suggested below. As people awaken more consciously to the messages contained within colour, there is a tendency for them to become more aware of their colour needs from day to day, particularly in regard to clothing. And while there is no need to spend a small fortune on redecorating the house and buying new sheets, nevertheless pictures, scatter cushions and ornaments all play a part. You can bring the living energies of plants and their blossoms into your living room and garden. Shops the world over are making striking use of colour in almost every gadget and ornament on the market.

Moreover, there are ways of bringing colour right into the energy field and the physical body which have a much deeper and more permanent effect even than these outer methods can achieve. You can take the knowledge of what colours you need and use any of these methods to bring that knowledge into your life in all sorts of ways as a force for change within yourself. Colour can have healing effects on all the different levels within you, including your physical health. Your physical health affects your emotional health; and both affect the quality of your relationships.

You can absorb the colour rays that you need through the food that you eat; or you can imbue your drinks with the energies of any ray under the sun. You can lace your bath with flower essences, essential oils, and coloured soaps and bath lotions, or even with natural dyes that colour the water in which you bathe. You can call on the services of professional therapists who offer colour counselling, chakra balancing through the use of coloured light, or colourpuncture, an exciting and revolutionary system of light medicine which immediately irradiates the cells through the meridians of the body. Here is a brief look at a few of these possibilities.

Colour in Food

The foods you eat provide one of the most obvious means by which you can absorb the energies of the colour rays you need. You are what you eat, and food is essentially the energies of colour materialised by the plant, or sometimes by the animal, depending on one's food habits and preferences. What happens is that plants take in the seven cosmic rays (i.e. Red, Orange, Yellow, Green, Blue, Indigo and Violet) from the light energy of the universe, and they then convert it, through the process of photosynthesis, into a form which they use to grow and to sustain life. You then set about to reverse this process when, in consuming these energies as the solid matter of plants, you break it down through the process of metabolism, eventually making it available to the body as energy in a form you can use. This process continues up the food chain, through animals to humankind. Human beings and animals, like plants, also absorb these cosmic rays directly through the skin and eyes; but, at this stage in evolution, this process is subsidiary to the process of digesting the food which is our chief source of energy. Paying attention to food, and its colour, is therefore a valuable aspect of any treatment involving colour.

At present, there is still relatively little which is widely known and accepted in the West about the exact combinations of the cosmic rays which should be absorbed through your food for perfect harmony and health. Both the Indians and the Chinese teach that all foods are composed not only of the seven rays of the spectrum, but also of the five elements: earth, water, air, fire and ether. Differences in the composition and quality of foods are attributed to the quality and quantity of these rays and elements, and dis-ease is attributed to the wrong combinations of foods as well as to the more obvious factors of over- or under-consumption.

There are perhaps two general principles, when paying attention to the colours in your foods, which are significant. One is the need for balancing different types (and colours) of foods, because not only do you need to attempt to balance the rainbow spectrum, but also Red, Orange and Yellow foods have an alkaline effect; Blue, Indigo and Violet foods have an acid effect; and Green foods are neither acid nor alkaline: Green helps to bring about balance in this as well as in other contexts. Being neutral, Green foods help to maintain the optimum pH balance.

The other general principle is to introduce the foods from the hotter and more energetic end of the spectrum – that is to say the Red, Orange and Yellow ones – towards the beginning of the day, and to reserve the calming ones – the Blues, Indigos and Violets – for the later hours.

In addition to these general principles, of course, your intake of specific foods can be increased, depending upon the seasonal availability, according to your needs. If, say, Yellow has emerged as an area of depletion, then it will help you to redress the imbalance in the solar plexus area if you drink lemon juice, eat fresh Yellow peppers in salads, and incorporate the foods of this ray into your meals throughout the day, not just in the morning. The Table on pages 87–90 listing some of the major foods associated with each of the chakra rays, may help in planning your colour diet.

THERAPEUTIC USE OF COLOUR

Colour is used in a number of ways by different forms of complementary therapy. One of the first people in modern times to recognise the therapeutic effect of colour was Rudolf Steiner, who harnessed the energies of colour in teaching patients the aesthetic laws of painting. He felt that, in learning the laws of colour, harmony, balance and rhythm, the individual learns to find balance within himself. He encouraged his patients to paint in the abstract mode, using water colours freely on large pieces of paper without any thought form or object. This therapy, which not only frees up a person's creativity but gives them a channel for the unconscious and suppressed aspects of their personality to express themselves, is highly satisfying, and nurturing, and therapeutic, for those with any inclination towards self-expression through paintbrushes.

Colour Baths

These are a very immediate and nurturing source of colour. This system was used in ancient cultures, and has been developed in contemporary times by Inger Naess in Norway. The bottles of colour contain natural, organic substances which are added to the bath water. The seven colours through from Red to Violet allow you to create exactly the tone, and the depth of colour, that you like. Total immersion in the colour ray of your choice allows your body to soak in and absorb the energy you need, and it can act as a powerful tonic. It is also very enjoyable. To enhance the beneficial effects of the colour, you can also add a few drops of the essential oil appropriate to the colour you have chosen (see Table on pages 89–92). For further details, you can visit the website given at the back of this book.

Solarised Water

You can energise the water you drink with any particular ray by placing it in a glass container of the required colour and exposing it to the sun for at least an hour. Ideally, it should then be gently sipped throughout the day, rather than being gulped down and finished within a short time.

Crystal or Gem Therapy

Gems and crystals have been collected as objects of beauty, made into jewellery, and even in some countries incorporated into the walls of palaces, throughout the ages. They are very useful in colour therapy because of the purity of their colour and the concentration of energy which they contain. Like plants, crystals grow within the earth. Unlike plants, they grow very slowly, deep within the bowels of the planet, where they expand and take shape over thousands of years, gradually absorbing the universal life force. They are, in fact, solidified light, each family of crystals being the purest materialisation of any one particular ray. Their energy is powerfully concentrated and very pure. There are numerous ways of using gems therapeutically: one simple method is to place the gem in water or alcohol for about a week and then to mix a drop of that fluid with water. This dilution has the effect of potentising the fluid, thereby producing a powerful remedy, which is then administered homoeopathically. Healers often administer advice on the appropriate gem for a person to wear or carry. Some of these crystals and gems are listed in the Table on pages 89–92 .

Essential Oils

These, like crystals, foods and flowers, are briefly listed in the Table on pages 89–92. Within the last couple of decades, aromatherapy, which is the remedial use of the concentrated oils from plants, has become widely recognised as a treatment which can achieve deep and lasting results, particularly in conjunction with massage for the relief of stress. It is a helpful way to make the vibration of the plant available to the physical body; and although the oils themselves are only "oil-coloured" or colourless except only for their variation in shade, they nevertheless contain the wavelength which is the essence of that plant and which expresses itself, among other ways, through the colour-signature which it displays in its blossom or its berries. Essential oils can also be absorbed by other means: through their use in the bath, through oil vaporisers which emit their vibration into the atmosphere, or simply sprinkled on a pillow.

N.B. Essential oils are very potent and care should be taken by pregnant mothers only to use these oils under the supervision of a qualified aromatherapist.

Flower Essences

Like essential oils, flower essences contain the characteristic vibration that corresponds to the plant of its origin, rather than themselves showing that plant's colour. When the plant is flowering and at the height of its power, the essence of the flower is carried into water. This is often done simply by bending the head of the flower into the water, usually in the presence of sunlight, which prevents any damage to the plant itself. It seems that this water is then able to hold an imprint of the plant's qualities, which is conveyed to you when you add a few drops of a flower essence to a glass of spring water and sip it. This is usually done two or three times a day over a period of several weeks. The essences of flowers are potent and subtle, acting gently on the whole of the energy system, and thus on your consciousness, to bring about a state of equilibrium.

Colour Ray Lamps

These are lamps which use a high-wattage bulb to transmit colour vibrations, such as Red, Orange, Yellow or whatever is appropriate, on to a particular area of the body. They are so constructed as to allow the easy insertion or removal of glass slides or filter papers. In average cases it is recommended that treatment be given once or twice a day; in severe cases it may be administered more often. This can be a powerful treatment, particularly when the more stimulating rays are used, and care should be taken not to overtreat.

Colourpuncture

The method of shining coloured lamps has been further developed in the innovation of Colourpuncture. This is a radical and exciting new medicine of light. In this system, coloured light is focussed most particularly on acupuncture points on the skin, and on other points as well, stimulating a powerful healing response in our physical and energetic bodies. This appears to be a remarkable way of sending healing messages throughout the body at the speed of light, which was founded and developed by the German scientist Peter Mandel. Colourpuncture has been thoroughly described in a book by Jack Allanach: *"It beams straight to afflicted cells with the harmonizing information inherent in colour – and the healing news is shouted from cell to cell"* (*Colour me Healing*, Jack Allanach, Element Books). Miraculous cures have been reported for imbalances on every level, physical, emotional, mental and spiritual, through the use of this therapy.

Colour Breathing

This is an easy method of bringing the ray you need into the energetic field and the body. It is done by breathing in the colour you wish to receive, either to the chakra to which it applies or into the whole of the body. In visualising the appropriate colour, and breathing it in and out, you can bring its energy speedily and directly to balance your physical and subtle bodies. It is also a particularly helpful tool for assisting other people. When used therapeutically by one person for another, this has in some cases brought about an instantaneous cure. The method may also be used in absent healing, where the colour vibrations are sent to the person by thought process rather than by having them in the healer's physical presence. The principle is the same as that used in the physical world in guided missiles, radio, television and radionics.

Colour breathing is a useful technique, as it can be used anywhere at any time. Within the context of our close relationships, it can be a powerful aid in providing support to a person in need, or in restoring harmony after a conflict. The appropriate ray in any situation becomes obvious once you have acquired a degree of familiarity with the meanings attached to various colours. If you know that someone has just received some kind of shock, for example, you can direct the Orange ray towards him on the breath. Blue, sent later, could then help him to find what communication he needs in order to begin the process of letting go of the shock and finding peace of mind. If something has caused conflict within the home or office, Pink directed towards the scene before you arrive will help all those involved, including of course yourself, in softening rough edges and creating an atmosphere of compassion and unconditional care.

The technique of colour breathing can be extended into the practices of visualisation and meditation. An Appendix at the back of the book gives a number of guided journeys, or visualisations, which can be used for these purposes.

Chakra Balancing

This is something practised by many healers who work with energy. Most people, however, have more facility than they realise for harnessing these energies for themselves. While guided visualisations may be used when you wish to access the strength of one particular ray, it is also very nurturing to work either on yourself or on each other in a partnership to balance the chakras. To do this, the most comfortable method is to lie horizontally, on a bed or a floor, with a small cushion under the head and another under the knees, and simply lay your hands on each of the energy stations in turn, starting with the pubic area and working up to the area above the crown. The chakra picture (Fig. 1, p. 97) shows the gradation of colours in relation to the areas of the body. At each energy station, visualise the appropriate-coloured energy moving through your hands. This is a wonderful exercise. Whether you do it on yourself or on another person, it leaves you (and the other person) feeling relaxed and refreshed. It can take as little as ten minutes or as long as an hour, depending on your need or the need of the person in question.

Aura-Soma

This school of colour therapy has already been mentioned several times through-out the text. Books are available which describe the system quite thoroughly (these include my own book, *Healing with Colour*, Element Books 1998). For this reason, only the briefest of descriptions is included here.

Aura-Soma has played a significant role in the return of colour therapy to the Western world, after a long time in history when it had been little used. It has drawn on ancient knowledge from a number of resources to compound the philosophy that underpins its method of working. The aim of this therapy is to assist the client in coming to a greater level of awareness. An Aura-Soma teacher or therapist guides individuals, through the mirror offered by their personal selections of colour, towards the kind of thorough knowledge of themselves which enables them to create their experience consciously rather than merely to react automatically to the circumstances that surround them. This method of empowering the individual therefore describes itself as a "self-selective, non-intrusive soul therapy". The core of the system is a range of about a hundred glass bottles containing two-coloured combinations of liquids. These are highly-coloured oils resting on a base of water, which are also attractively coloured, generally in a different hue from the one above. In the same way that this book has invited you to choose your favourite colours, the client coming to an Aura-Soma consultation is offered the choice of four colour combinations from the entire range. The counsellor is trained to interpret the meaning of this selection; and through the messages that the client's choice of colour brings, to help the client to recognise the significant issues raised. Aura-Soma also manufacture a range of coloured products, so that it is possible to reinforce the information gleaned from the colours chosen in a practical way.

• • • • •

This briefly summarises some of the chief methods currently available for harnessing the energies of colour to alter your consciousness, your state of health, and ultimately the health of your relationships. They can be used separately or concurrently to support you in your journey into colour and to offer you the maximum benefit and enjoyment from the rays you need, or love, the most.

chapter 13

FROM DARK AGES TO LIGHT YEARS AHEAD

Already, in the silence of the night, I can hear through this world of tumult a confused rustling as of crystalline needles forming themselves into a pattern or of birds huddling closer together in their nest – a deep murmur of distress, of discomfort, of well-being, of triumph, rising up from the Unity which is reaching its fulfilment.

Pierre Teilhard de Chardin

The Great Monad

Your central relationships are like the hub of the wheel whose movement generates and influences all your experiences, inner and outer. Depending on their quality and health, they can drive you towards the deepest joys and the fulfilment of all that is greatest and best in your intentions, or they can grind you to a juddering halt. Your relationships, just like everything else, need to be maintained and serviced. The regular cleaning and lubricating of these is as vital to your fulfilment and happiness as is the good care of your body to your health, or the attention to household chores to the harmonious running of your home.

Where a relationship is dysfunctional, the damming up of the energy flow affects everything within and around you, from the way you feel when you get up in the morning to the health of your monthly bank statement; from your performance at work to whether your children sleep at night. Whatever is discordant within your relationships will, inevitably and precisely, reverberate upon the condition of all that surrounds you. Unhappy relationships create inefficiency, poverty and ill health. There is every reason in the world why it is worth doing all you can to look at what it is in your own experience that is barring your way to an abundance of health and wealth on every level, and to the free flowing of love.

The intuition is often way out in front of the intellect. It is certainly true that much of the inspiration in the world has come through channels other than those of reason: music and art, systems for healing, and even some of the world's great inventions have been born through meditation or dreams. For centuries, the healing energies of colour were recognised and understood only through intuition or by mystics. Colour is the expression of light, and while there is much still to be discovered about its mysteries, science is making quantum leaps in its discovery of how intimately our physiology and our consciousness is bound up with light. Contemporary science, in fact, is able to offer some explanation of what mystics, working with faculties beyond the intellect, have known and practised for hundreds, and sometimes thousands, of years. Research is unveiling the secret language of our cells, as they flash their colour-coded messages to and fro. It is constantly pushing the frontiers of our knowledge, as it discovers the role played by light in communication – both on earth and between the planets. This is merely the tip of the iceberg. These pages have demonstrated to you something of how you are in constant communication with all those around you, through the quality of your thoughts and feelings and expectations, which is translated through the energy field around you into the colour of the light that you radiate. This communication is happening at the level of the aura: the ancient knowledge of this process must soon combine with science to pave the way towards a new understanding of the powerful means by which we constantly communicate with one another – at the speed of light – long before, or after, we have even heard or spoken a word!

If the universe exists as the consequence of the light energy which exploded in the "big bang", this is not a process that happened once and is now complete. This light energy continues to move and to expand, constantly forming and re-forming everything that we experience as the living world. This includes ourselves: our bodies, our feelings, our thoughts; at some level, our consciousness itself. Everything, in fact, has consciousness. This is demonstrated by experiment with the nature of light, which has shown that it will behave either as a particle or as a wave, according to the *expectation of the observer*. In some way, every particle in the universe is interconnected. This in turn means that even our thoughts have an influence on the universe with which we interact. Perhaps the first way in which they express themselves is in their immediate impact on the colour of the aura surrounding us. We communicate with each other on the inner as well as the outer planes. Our thoughts, even our most unconscious ones, are not merely abstract: they could be described as packages of energy. They travel around like waves or particles in the air and they are picked up by others who are receptive to them; in other words, part of how we communicate is through the power of thought, which is transmitted via particles of light. It is as though a secret postal or telecommunications network carries our thoughts, our feelings, and our expectations to precisely the address or number where it is most appropriate for them to be received; and then exactly the message we need, in the form of an opportunity or an experience, comes bounding back to us. All of this can happen, not surprisingly, at the speed of light!

How often have we talked of being *"in the dark"* about things of which we have either been uninformed or which we have not understood? Difficulties that have not been processed do not simply go away: they remain with us and sit like hooks, so to speak, in the aura; waiting for someone to come and hang stuff up on them. Have you ever heard of hang-ups? Well, that is exactly what they are: all the conscious and all the unconscious feelings of fear, anger, guilt, confusion, jealousy, possessiveness, untruth; plus all the rest of our unfinished business. It hovers, *"hung up"* in the aura of most of us like a fog on a November morning. It prevents us from seeing clearly, and thus has an immediate effect on our communication; it weighs us down; and it takes us out of our balance. And then, this repercusses on us in all sorts of uncomfortable ways, including our relationships and our state of health. But it is only the negative states which build up this fog. Positive states, such as unconditional love, joy, enthusiasm, peace, generosity, humour, truthfulness, and many others, give added light and clarity to the aura. Through working with colour, you can dispel this fog and create a new clarity. It is exactly this clarity that you need to aim at if you want to nurture your communications. The

> *It is exactly this clarity that you need to aim at if you want to nurture your communications.*

clearer you are about your own needs, motives, feelings and thoughts, the harder it is to fail to communicate those things clearly to the people you love. An Eastern mystic, Yogaswami, has expressed this very simply: *"Running water will run faster if you remove an obstruction here and there. You need not do much more."*

So your aura, and indeed your mind, needs clearing on a regular basis. If you use a computer a lot, do you find, like I do, that every so often your hard disc gets stuffed full of unnecessary documents? Does it begin hobbling along like an old man with a walking stick, and perhaps even jumble up the instructions it receives? Dodging in and out from behind the documents that you need are a whole lot more, older ones; or perhaps a load of the sticking and pasting that happens as you attempt to make sense of what you have written by re-assembling it, just as we do in life. It all gets scrambled and it *takes up unnecessary space*. This jumble affects the communication between you and your machine. The computer is so cluttered with fog that it becomes dense and slow. It has to be cleaned up. All the documents, all the odd particles, that you no longer need have to be swept away; and then all of a sudden, it moves at lightning speed again. This image is a simplification of what can happen in our minds and hearts; but you get the picture.

Colour is an extraordinary tool. It is a reflector of the gentlest and most profound nature, penetrating deep into the furthest reaches of human consciousness and bringing up long-suppressed memories which otherwise fester until they express themselves in uncomfortable, often painful ways. Colour has a depth and breadth of insight to teach you about the various ways in which you relate to those who are near and dear to you: the specific challenges which you have to work through in your friendships or partnerships in order to understand yourself and one another better; the potential within these very difficulties to become the means towards your greatest strengths, and the often unrecognised gifts which you have and may share with one another.

Our experience in between the two momentous events of our birth and our death is essentially a social one, and the deepest desire in most of us is to relate to those we love or like in a creative and harmonious way: to overcome the duality that divides us in order that we may know and be known; understand and be understood; love and be loved. An understanding of your own and another's colours will enable you to leave behind the isolation of a polarised past and to look at where it is that you are going. Your eyes can be opened to the possibilities of where you *can* go, together. You can move from division towards a unity that is more real than it would have been without the experience of having been divided.

In other words your very conflicts can become the food that fuels your journey towards true intimacy and a deeper unity. As the "*hang-ups*" are cleared, little by little, from your aura and thus from your heart and mind, the polarities within you and between you soften. As you sit more comfortably with yourself, you also become more aware of your complementarity with a friend or partner than of your conflicts; you move beyond division and into a deeper unity. Like ice and steam that appear so different at first glance, but whose watery essence is a shared one, you too can discover, through your shared essence of colour and light, that both your source and your destiny are closer than they have often appeared to be.

The polarity that has kept the human race divided has existed since the dawn of time, when light first emerged out of the void of darkness. It is an inevitable phenomenon in a material universe. A young English soldier was shocked and distressed to find inscribed on the belt of another young, German soldier whom he had just killed, the words "*God is on our side*". This shattered him and turned his world upside down: his teaching had been effective in convincing him that it was the English side that God had favoured. This is the ultimate example of polarity: a situation where, through the collective fear that comes from our failure to understand where another person, or society, is coming from, we kill before we come to realise that ultimately we were coming from the same belief, or place. As we work with colour, we can become more conscious of its essential oneness. Every colour, in the final analysis, is merely an aspect of the White light that is universal. Similarly, every creature on this planet comes from the same source as, and is interconnected with, every other living thing.

Colour is the manifestation of light in our world. To find an understanding of colour is to find a route back towards the love from which we came. It offers us the means to recognise the beauty not only within all the life around us but also within ourselves, so that we can approach those around us from a place not of poverty but of limitless abundance. Love is the original and natural state: the creative source which gave rise to both the darkness and the light.

Our most intimate relationships, ultimately, should serve as the model for all the relationships in our lives. The possibilities for working with colour beyond the confines of our families and intimate friendships are infinite. We can look at our relationships at work, bringing colour into corporate management. Such a tool will not only help us to resolve industrial and management conflicts, but will hugely increase productivity as energy becomes redirected towards a more fruitful end. What are the possibilities within our prisons, our police force and our hospitals? What are the opportunities within our schools and universities, as teachers come to a new recognition and sense of responsibility for themselves? How much better equipped could they become, through the illumination provided by an understanding of colour and light, to take on the responsibility for guiding a new generation on the winding road towards maturity? What are the implications for world co-operation and peace, as we – and even world governments – look towards one another in a spirit of openness and love for what we can learn, and share, rather than in a spirit of fear for what we should fight about?

Perhaps deep within the memory bank of us all is some dim recollection of our original state of unity and perfect balance, before duality was created and separateness came about. The ultimate polarity is that of heaven and earth, spirit and matter. To bridge this duality is to find the route towards our deepest creativity: to enhance the quality of all that we do, moment to moment, day to day. To access this in ourselves is to discover a great gift. It is the light at the very centre of ourselves, the still point at the centre of the hurricane, which is the divinity within ourselves. Through the energies of colour and light, we can find illumination for the fears that have previously blocked our understanding, so that we may transcend our duality and find the road back to love. Colour, the expression of the multi-faceted energy of light, takes us back to the very beginning. Through colour, we can gain not only an understanding of our own nature and the workings of the subconscious, but we can find ways of enjoying the differences between us all as something that enrich us rather than threaten us.

The final pages of this chapter were written on the last Remembrance Sunday of the millennium. Representatives from one third of the countries in the world gathered on this day to pay their respects to the millions of young men who were killed or maimed in the wars of the twentieth century. At the end of this occasion, it was suggested that whether or not war continues into the next century, and beyond, will depend upon the youth of the next generation. This is incomplete. It depends upon every one of us: it depends upon the degree to which every human being is prepared to acknowledge our responsibility for what we create. When we own our shadow, our darkness, as well as our light, we can dispense with illusion and communicate in truth: not just with our spouses or our closest friends, but on a vastly greater scale. We shall stop sacrificing the lives of others for the preservation of our freedom, because ultimately it is only the truth that has the power to set us free.

Ideals are like stars: you will not succeed
in touching them with your hands. But like
the seafaring man on the desert water,
you choose them as your guides, and,
following them you will reach your destiny.
Carl Schurz

Guided Visualisations in Colour

What if you slept? And what if in your sleep, you dreamed?
And what if in your dream you went to heaven and there plucked
a strange and beautiful flower?
And what if, when you awoke, you had the flower in your hand?
Ah! What then?

Samuel Taylor Coleridge

These guided visualisations, or journeys, are available on a set of audio cassette tapes: to listen to these visualisations rather than to read them is perhaps an easier and more effective method of absorbing the resonance they contain. However, they are included here for easy reference in case you would like to dip into any of the colours you want to work with.

Visualisation is a powerful means of accessing the energies of colour, which can take you into a deep state of relaxation. This must therefore be done in circumstances where it is quite safe to let to go completely of any job in hand, and to relax. Never do this when driving a car or operating machinery of any kind. The visualisations are given in the order in which the colours appear in the spectrum, from Red at one end through to the Violet and Magenta at the other end, and finally to White.

Each time you embark on a guided *"journey"* into the colour of your choice, find a time when you can be confident that there will be no outside demands; if possible, switch off the phone for a short while. Choose a quiet space where you can spend ten minutes to half an hour undisturbed, and either sit up straight or lie on your back. Some people like to hold, or place on the appropriate chakra, a crystal or gem that resonates with the colour of any particular visualisation: Clear Quartz, for example, may potentise the energy of a journey through the clear or White energy; Lapis Lazuli, the Indigo one; Emerald or Malachite, the Green.

Whichever colour energy you are working with, prepare yourself for a few minutes first by bringing your full attention to the movement of the breath, as it travels rhythmically in and out of your lungs. As you concentrate more deeply on this movement, you will begin to notice a softening throughout your body, so that the breath seems to move, not just into your lungs, but into the deeper parts of your abdomen, and even into your limbs. Then begin to notice how it feels to breathe outwards. On each out-breath, encourage your body to let go of some of those things it habitually holds. The key to this is in the areas that feel tight: it is in the very cells of our bodies that we store our thoughts and feelings and discomfort and pain. Notice how each out-breath is a little deeper than the last one, leaving behind it a cleaner and emptier space. Then, simply wait until the next breath starts to arrive, and allow it to enter, massaging the diaphragm and the abdominal organs as it moves. Feel your body become heavier and soft, as areas of tension begin, little by little, to loosen up.

RED

It is a hot summer afternoon. You are walking barefoot through a field blazing with scarlet poppies. Feel the contact of your feet with the soil: your heels, the balls of your feet, and your toes. Feel the Red energy that throbs and circulates within the body of the earth, rising to burst into all the life we see on her surface. Just as Red blood carries the energy around our bodies, so the energy of the earth is Red. It is vital; free-flowing. Notice how this gentle earth throb feels as your feet make contact with the ground. Imagine the life that is hidden inside the body of the planet: the animals and all the insects; the roots of trees and plants; the Red rubies and garnets which grow infinitely slowly deep inside the bowels of the earth, absorbing and crystallising the purest energies of the Red ray. The movement of the colour Red is like the rising of the ocean swell, passionate and powerful, travelling onwards and outwards with grace and strength. It urges us to move forward with the flow. As you walk, allow the poppies to brush against the tips of your fingers: feel the Redness of the flower in your hands. Walk on, as the poppy field gives way to an area of open land. What you feel here underfoot is no longer soft earth, but warm stones, massaging and pummelling your toes and the balls of your feet. Notice how the Red energy moves, as your feet awaken, through your legs, moving on and up, just as far as the base of the pelvis. Suffused now by Redness, your feet, your legs, your hips and your hands feel the gentle heat rising through them, like warm Red wine coursing through your veins. Warm and relaxed, you lie down now, feeling this Redness as, with each inward breath, the radiance deepens. As you breathe out, your body relaxes more deeply, letting its weight be supported by the earth below. Trust the earth to hold you as you focus only on the glowing Red which fills and strengthens your feet and legs, your hips and hands. Your hands feel warm. Maybe they tingle a little. Your toes feel alive and awake in the relaxation spreading right through your body. You feel as graceful as a cat soaking up the warmth of the sun: completely relaxed and fully alert. As you feel the rising of this strength, you feel newly and more firmly connected to your physical body. You know that when you choose to come out of this state of relaxation, all your faculties will be awake and alert, ready to bring to earth whatever ideas move you. Your feet are your understanding. Thank your feet and your hands for the connection they give you to the earth which is your home.

After five or ten minutes, or as long as feels comfortable, watch as the Red gently subsides, leaving you restored and energised. Rest a while longer if you wish, and when you are ready to do so, take a few long deep breaths and bring your body back into normal consciousness, knowing that your two feet are firmly connected with the ground.

PINK

Pink is the colour of childhood, and femininity, and soft intuitive warmth. When we "*think Pink*", we create around us an aura of well-being. See this Pink light around you; feel it; and begin to breathe it in towards you as you inhale. Through the Pink ray, you can regain your connection with the new-born being within; with the child who was once so open and trusting. That child may have hidden itself away, building thick walls in the hope of protecting itself from the pain of any more wounds. Now feel yourself wrapped in a downy soft, feather-light blanket of Pink, rocking in the arms of a warm, strong being who loves you. This may be your mother; it may be a friend; perhaps it is a deceased relative, a spirit guide or an angel. Feel the warmth of the love that radiates from their arms and hands. Notice the gentleness of their face and the softness of their breath. The colour of all this love is Pink, and as you feel it your body begins to relax, inside and out, in its steady embrace. Your head, your neck, your spine are totally supported. The eyes that gaze at you express awe at the beauty and the gift of the life that is yours. The love that radiates from the face and the arms that hold you attaches no conditions: it is total; accepting and supporting you, loving you, every finger and toe, exactly the way things are. As you breathe in, accept this love. Allow the Pink that is its expression to permeate the cells of your body, running gently through you with a warm, fluid, translucent glow. Feel it move through your body, head to toe, filling your arms and legs and hands and feet. The Pink ray awakens and energises the whole body, bringing it to life as a bud is brought to flower in the warmth of the sun. Allow the Pink to settle in the lower abdomen, the area of the womb, where man or woman can feel the colour as it expands. Just as the womb extends itself to make room for each new life, so the Pink here makes a space for the child within yourself.

For as long as it feels comfortable, feel and watch this Pink light which suffuses your body. Allow it to offer you the conditions you need so that, like a young and tender plant, you can firm up your trunk and grow upwards towards the light. Know that when you choose to return to your normal, fully waking state, the blanket of Pink protective warmth will remain with you if you wish it to, softening the energy around you to create a gentler reality within your daily life. When you feel ready to return to normal consciousness, take a few deep breaths, feel the floor beneath you, and open your eyes.

CORAL

You are lying in a small boat on a warm still sea. Above you is a clear sky; in the distance is a landscape full of sunshine and exotic fruits and flowers; beneath you, the ocean runs deep. Around you is perfect silence, interrupted only occasionally by the sound of a sea bird. Turning yourself over in the boat, you find its glass base showing you a glimpse of an unknown world within the sea. You want to plumb those depths. Gently you climb into the water and let yourself sink down. At first you are surrounded by a cloudy wetness; as you go deeper and deeper, the water around you begins to clear. If you feel the need for air, know you can access an oxygen mask whenever you want it. Otherwise know that, for the present, the element of water offers all that you need. The sea feels friendly and warm. You move further into its depths, delighting in the texture of the warm water as it moves around your hands and feet and caresses the surfaces of your body. Now you see the ocean bed: reefs of rich, peachy-coloured Coral. The colour surrounds you and suffuses you, filling the cells of your body with a gentle warmth. The stones of the ocean floor are soft as apricots and smooth as eggs. Gently you sit on this floor; your body weightless as the water supports it. All around you is the Coral, which hardly moves at all, and the sea plants, which move gently with the slight motion of the water. Within this circle of Coral, you feel perfectly protected and absolutely safe. You sit, quite still, surrounded by quiet movement and perfect peace. Little by little, you become aware of gentle sea creatures moving towards you and caressing you before they slide silently away. Others come to offer you gifts. Each of them brings you the same assurance of love and warmth: the knowledge that what you need will be provided. All around, and through your body, you feel the warmth of the Coral ray as it floods your feelings, your thoughts and your cells.

Allow yourself to bask within this Coral ray, on the ocean bed, until your body feels warmed and nourished by its sustenance. Feel it within the lower part of your abdomen, connecting you with your intuition and your wisdom. You may stay on the ocean floor until you choose to return. You know that when you feel replete and wish to return to normal consciousness, you can swim upwards towards White light and air, and a landscape of luscious plants and birds of paradise. Full and relaxed, take a few deep breaths, stretch your limbs, and open your eyes.

ORANGE

Orange is the warmth of the fireside hearth, bringing us right home; and it is also the fiery glow of sunset, lending us the aspiration to look upwards and outwards and reach for the stars. Look for a while, then, at a warm fire in the grate, and watch the Orange glow of the embers radiant in their heat. Feel the warmth of that fire spread through the lower part of your body, and notice how the inner organs respond to its heat, vitality and joy. Orange is the sun-rich food that vitalises our bodies, and it is the autumn leaves that surrender their physical life to offer their nourishment to a new cycle. As you sit beside the Orange glow of the hearth, take a long slow breath inwards, and feel this ray as it fills the deepest part of your body: a warm fluid energy running through the gut; a gentle heat that softens all it touches. Like a monk of Tibet, feel yourself wrapped all around by the warmth and joy of an Orange robe. Taste the juice of fresh oranges and exotic fruits; feel their nourishment as their liquid flame warms and penetrates the deepest entrails of your being.

On the outward breath, feel the Orange as it begins to surround the rest of your body: a cloud of warmth, uplifting and inspiring. Now, supported and protected by this cloud, allow yourself to be wafted to the edge of a cliff in the setting sun. The air is warm and balmy. The sky on the horizon glows Orange around the perfect sphere, the light of the fiery sun. You can look directly at this light. Its fierce mid-day brilliance has subsided. Feel the Orange ray, now, as it rests within your abdomen, helping you to absorb the experiences of the day, just as the earth has absorbed the warmth of the sun. Watch as its fluid nature washes away the residue of all these experiences: the Orange is the roughage which keeps you active and carries away the surplus, to be used for something else. Accept the help of the Orange ray in letting go of all that you no longer need. The colour moves on down, deeper and deeper into the gut, taking with it the shocks and traumas of the past, leaving you with only the learning as the pain evaporates and disappears. The Orange transports you deep into the wisdom of your own inner voice. All you sense now is stillness: warmth, silence, and bliss.

Stay within this Orange space for as long as you wish to. Then, gently watch as the ray evaporates, merging into the rest of the White light that is all around you. Take a few long breaths, deep into the abdomen, ensuring that you feel firmly connected with the ground beneath you, before you open your eyes.

GOLD

It is a Golden day at the height of summer. You are walking beside crops that are coming into their time of harvest Gold: corn and barley, rye and wheat. Everywhere is warm and glowing. Take some deep breaths and feel as the Gold energy floods down through your lungs and into the solar plexus below, filling the area just below the navel with a soft Golden glow. Feel the gentle sensation as this light floods your cells, bringing warmth and relaxation to the centre of your body; the area around your navel opening gently like a bud, expanding into full flower, to receive the nourishment, the life force directly from the sun. Notice how that Golden light radiates gently from the sun centre of your own body, upwards, downwards, inwards, outwards.

As you walk slowly on, you arrive at a gorge overlooking a Golden valley below. Move on down towards the valley, breathing in the Golden energy as you go, until you come to an entrance on the side of this gorge which leads to a cave within. You know that you are welcome here; and so you go inside to explore. As you feel the walls of this cave with the backs of your hands, you realise they are coated with Gold leaf, glistening and smooth. Little by little, your eyes become accustomed to the relative darkness of the cave. Softly softly, Golden treasures begin to appear before your eyes: a Golden throne, a crown, jewels of great value and beauty. These are treasures of the earth; but as Gold is rich on the earth plane, so it is rich in spirit. It is pure and deeply protective. You feel quite safe here; and as you contemplate these works of art, you discover that what you are meeting are the jewels inside yourself: your wisdom, your certainty, your knowledge, your joy. Go deep inside this place. Take the Golden light and watch as it illumines that store-place of wisdom and understanding. Feel the joy of certainty as you realise that the key to your destiny lies within your own centre, safely housed and protected until each moment when you choose to take it out, to open a door to the next pathway in your life.

Hold this Gold light within and around the sun centre of your being for as long as it feels comfortable, before allowing it to return to the universal life force from where it came. If you choose to keep it with you, simply allow this Gold light to stay within the solar plexus. Take a few more deep breaths, feel the firm foundation of the earth beneath you, and open your eyes.

YELLOW

It is a mild day in early spring. The Yellow sun is warm and bright and fresh; the sky is clear. You are sitting in a small cottage garden, shielded on all sides from wind, and surrounded by the Yellow flowers of springtime: daffodils, crocuses, primroses, all lifting their heads to the sun's warmth, and a new season. Like egg yolks and chickens, the Yellow ray celebrates the joy and the miracle of the self-renewing cycle of life.

As you take some inward breaths, you feel inside you the refreshing quality of the Yellow ray. It travels straight to the nerve centre of your system, around the area of the navel. The "spaghetti junction" of the nerve centre, this area may sometimes have felt a little tight. The Yellow light flows through the cells here, bringing a fluid freshness like the juice of lemons, clearing confusion, bringing a new flow of energy. Feel the clarity of these rays of sunshine, within your own centre and all around; bringing a sharp luminescence to all that it touches. Spring is a time to be reborn; a time for cleaning out the cupboards; clearing away the dross of our lower natures and our petty concerns, so we can see the fuller picture. Feel the cleansing rejuvenating quality of the Yellow.

Notice a new sense of your individual strength as your solar plexus centre clears and opens itself to receive this ray. The Yellow brings knowledge and understanding. It clears out fear and anxiety, replacing it with the confidence and certainty we feel on a warm sunny day. Yellow, breathed deeply into the solar plexus, gives you the courage and clarity to be yourself. Notice the happiness of the new life that both surrounds you and penetrates your centre. Know yourself to be part of this flow; and also a separate and unique entity: one piece of the jigsaw of life without which the picture would be incomplete. Allow yourself to be fully in this moment, "*full of the joys of spring*", as you bask in the light and the warmth of the sun's new rays.

Hold this Yellow space within and around the solar plexus until you feel your whole body being uplifted and refreshed. When you feel that your body has accepted all the Yellow energy that it requires for the moment, allow this ray to move back and rejoin the White light that is its closest relation. Know that at any moment that you wish to do so, you can rekindle this Yellow light inside you merely by thinking about it. Bring your attention back once more to the breath, and to the earth that supports your weight. Take a few deep breaths and when you feel ready, open your eyes.

OLIVE GREEN

As you breathe in the colour Olive Green, take your attention to the area between your solar plexus and your heart. See the Olive ray and watch as it moves deeply through your heart and lungs, to penetrate the area just below. You are walking, now, in a forest, on the softest mossy earth. Your feet are bare. The ground is soft and fresh, like a Green carpet. The newest of leaves are just appearing on the trees, after a winter that has been long and hard. Look at the leaves as some of them are beginning to unfurl, offering the promise of a new cycle, a renewed opportunity. These leaves are a pale and delicate Olive Green hue: fragile yet determined; full of hope and trust.

The forest leads you on. Apart from quietly absorbing the beauty of new growth, you have no desire to stop. You are on a journey; you have a sense of direction and purpose, the desire to lead yourself on to fertile pastures and to discover what is new. Soon, you arrive at a bridge. This bridge, too, is moss-covered. Your feet enjoy the firm connection with the earth, feeling the energy of that earth almost as a plant feels its roots. In the centre of this bridge, you stop for the first time. Below the bridge, a river runs smoothly and purposefully. Gazing into the water, you see how willing it is to accept the pain and bitterness from the past that has been held within your heart, and to wash it downstream towards the great sea: the sea of universal consciousness, which will understand and transmute this pain. As you breathe out, the Olive ray carries with it the old burdens and old pains, so the heart begins to feel lighter.

The Olive bridge on which you stand is the bridge between different dimensions of yourself. It is the path that enables you to leave behind the fears and anxieties of the past; the confusions about your value and your place; the bitterness endured by your heart. The Olive Green all around you, within you, and underfoot, allows you to move forward with grace and strength into a world where you know your wisdom and your purpose. The river carries away these old concerns: the Olive Green bridge leads you on to a new place of meeting with your heart, your own centre of truth and trust and hope; and outwards to the wider world. Confident, now, in the leadership you offer to yourself, you bring with you to this wider world the wisdom and compassion to understand its concerns and appreciate its gifts.

Allow yourself to remain on this Olive bridge, cleansed and refreshed by the running water below, until your heart and lungs feel strong and firm. When you feel that your need for this ray is satisfied, leave the Olive Green and the bridge behind you and allow the light around you to return to the normal White light of day, knowing that the bridge remains, strong and firm and ever-present for any future visits. Bring your attention back to the breath, and to the sensations of your body, in the knowledge that you are sitting or lying firmly supported by the floor beneath you. Take a few deep breaths, stretching to open wide your lungs and heart, and open your eyes.

GREEN

Green, above all the other colours, offers you space. You are lying in an open field. The air is fresh and warm. Feel the Greenness of the new grass beneath you. Feel its texture with your fingers, and as you breathe inwards, see and feel the quality of the fresh Green ray which enters your lungs and heart. Take your attention to your chest, watching the slow and steady Green movement as the breath moves in and out, like the tide that rolls forward and away again on the seashore. Allow your chest the space to expand into this Greenness, and notice how your heart and your lungs feel with this new-found space around them. The Green light flows right through your heart, right through your lungs: fluid Emerald, reminding you of your beauty and your truth. As this part of your body begins to expand and relax, it is followed by the other organs, the glands, and the limbs. Your whole body begins to feel heavy as it lets go and sinks into the support of the Green grass, trusting the earth, trusting the flow of life.

Lying in the grass, you are aware of the gentlest rustling sounds: you notice that around you, here and there, are large Green trees, standing well spaced and apart from one another: old oaks, smooth beeches, tall ashes; and young willows, bowing gracefully as they stoop towards the earth below. The trees are strong, patient, infinitely still. It is this Green stillness and strength that brings the birds towards them to build their nests. Rooted to the earth, they know that they cannot move. And so they live, in their Greenness, each moment; they watch, and wait, and accept. Like the tree, feel the connection of your body with the Green grass below; feel your roots pressing down into the earth, and the rising of the energy from the body of the earth, just as the sap rises in the trees.

Just for the moment, there is nowhere you have to go; nothing you have to do. Take this moment, and the Green ray, to be. Allow the Green hue to bring you to your inner truth, so that your heart may lead you. Open-hearted now, trust that you know your own way forward. You know your direction and your path; your deepest truth. The Green shows you trust and offers you hope. It is the promise of a new space and a new place.

Receive all that you need from the Green ray, breathing it deep into your body, accepting its soothing balm as it fills the space around you, for as long as you feel the need. When you feel relaxed and replete, allow the Green to dissipate into the atmosphere around you if you wish it to, returning gradually to the source of White light from where it came. If you feel a need for direction or space in your life at this time, it might help to keep this ray around you for a while. Take a few deep breaths to expand once more the chest, stretching out your arms and hands, and when you wish to do so, open your eyes.

TURQUOISE

Turquoise is a colour that talks of widespread, creative communication. It is the colour of the Aquamarine and the dolphin, of Turquoise gems. It links us with the art of ancient tribes whose telepathic awareness had no need of machines to ensure their wide and heartfelt communications. Feel the area in your chest above your heart and lungs. As you breathe in, see the colour Turquoise and watch it wash around the upper chest, as your heart area expands and finds communication with the throat. This is the inner being finding the freedom of the outer world as it gets to know itself.

Turquoise can travel easily. Breathe in this ray and feel your body becoming lighter and freer. See a Turquoise ocean and feel your body, like a dolphin or a fish, darting hither and thither, smoothly and gracefully, in the freedom of the water. Here you can play, leaving behind you the chores and the daily routine which sometimes seem to limit your expression. Here, in an ocean of Turquoise, you can feel the feelings of the other beings who share that space, frolicking, revelling, being. See the freedom of the sky, and feel the flight of birds who travel light as air. Supported by the Turquoise ray, we can adapt ourselves to meet whatever comes: feel the rising strength of your system of immunity, seated within the upper chest, as its Turquoise quality opens and flexes, ever-willing to bend and receive what is new.

As your body begins to experience this sense of freedom in the Turquoise ray, you notice again the expansion of the upper chest, as your heart finds its way to its expression. The gift within the Turquoise is to find communication for the feelings; through the expression of these feelings, there is the possibility for the deepest discovery of who you are. Turquoise is the colour of music, of poetry, of drama and all artistic form. Breathe in this ray and, through it, give birth to whatever it is that you wish to bring into the world. Turquoise is the inner teacher; that aspect of yourself that takes responsibility for whatever it is that you create. This is your truest freedom.

Stay with the Turquoise for as long as you wish, playing with the creatures of the air or the sea, giving vent to the expression of the heart. If you feel that for the moment you have no further need of this ray, let it move away from you to rejoin the White light that is its source. Take a few deep breaths, and bring your awareness back to the floor on which you are lying or sitting. Notice the weight of your body, and feel a firm connection with the earth before, in your own time, you open your eyes.

BLUE

You are seated beside the perfect stillness of a Blue lagoon. The sky above is the Blue of sapphires; the lagoon the Blue of the Madonna. Blue is the colour that brings you protection, trust and peace. As you gaze into the lagoon, and at the sky above, bring the Blue on the inward breath towards your throat. Notice how the Blue of the breath feels as it moves through your nose, down through your cheeks and face, and over your throat into the organs of speech. Feel the peaceful quality of this Blue ray, and allow it to soften everything that it touches, as each new inhalation brings you the breath of life. Feel a softening in the whole of your throat, and in anything you may wish to say, as the Blue brings to that area the possibility of clearer, more peaceful communication. If you become aware of any constrictions within the throat area, simply concentrate the Blue energy particularly on that place.

As you breathe out, notice the peacefulness of the Blue, and allow it to fill the space around you, so that the whole of your body becomes surrounded by a Blue light. This is like the Blue that surrounds the earth, gently allowing in all that is positive, while protecting it from those sun rays, or any other vibrations, that might be harmful. Within this space, you can let go of thoughts and feelings, taking this moment to allow the Blue ray to permeate your consciousness, filling your whole being with the feeling of faith and peace. Blue connects you with the energy of heaven, with the will of the Divine. Here, just for the moment, you have no need to be of any earthly use. There is nothing waiting to be done, nowhere that you have to go. You can simply receive. Here, too, you can let go of the shrill demands of the ego, in the knowledge that it is the greater plan that offers you true creativity and peace of mind.

With the support of the Blue ray, you can discover the strength in which you can stand alone. This is not loneliness: it is the peacefulness of unity with the whole created world; it is the serenity that overcomes the need to lean on others and allows you to be at one with yourself. Drink the Blue down deep. Allow it to permeate your body until you feel as peaceful and still as the lagoon and the sky.

When you feel it is time to return to earth and, perhaps, to action, bring your attention once more back to the breath. Watch the Blue turn back to the pure White light of day, or keep it around yourself for protection. Know, anyway, that you can call on it at any time you feel the need. As you breathe, notice the gentle weight of the breath in and out, and the physical sensation of your body weighing on the floor beneath you. Allow the energy to move downwards through your body, connecting you firmly with the earth. When you feel ready, open your eyes.

INDIGO

This is a colour of mystery and surprises: the colour of the sky as it moves from the day into the night. Indigo is the colour of sudden revelation, the flash of inspiration that comes in the darkest hour. This deep Blue is a royal colour. As you take some inward breaths, feel this Indigo ray travel towards the upper part of your head. Notice its power and its strength. Feel it swimming around your forehead, your eyes, your temples, your ears. The Indigo Blue brings with it the possibility of deep seeing, deep feeling, deep hearing. It is a colour that awakens you and lifts you to new levels of perception and understanding.

You are flying, gliding through the Indigo sky as day turns to night and the stars are switched on, one by one, like little electric lights, decorating the sky. All around you is the thought and the feeling of the Indigo ray. You can breathe it and you can touch it. The moon is full and bright, shining its light on the land of inspiration and dreams. The stars are just a hint of what lies beneath the surface of the mind; little lights offering a glimpse of the fertile land of the unconscious. Here, in the Indigo sky of the night, you can glimpse at some of those treasures stored within that land. The galaxies in our universe and beyond are expanding; their potential is infinite. The Indigo washes through you and around you, reminding you that your creative possibilities, like the universe itself, are unlimited. The constrictions that limit the achievements of your day are lifted in the Indigo of this night-time sky. This is the land of your dreams, where you can fly, where you can be all at once on earth and in heaven. Go deep into the Indigo; allow it to melt away the blocks that slow your vision and your hearing. Indigo is a catalyst which can bring swift and deep transformation to your perceptions and your thoughts.

When you feel that you have no further need of this ray for the moment, take a few long deep breaths, deep into the abdomen. Bring your attention back to the consciousness of the day; as the Indigo light melts back into the daylight that surrounds you, feel the earth beneath your legs and back; touch the floor with your hands. When you are ready, open your eyes.

VIOLET

Violet is the most calming of all the rays. Feel it now as it moves gently into the space around you. It is quiet and soothing, bringing peace to the body and the spirit. This colour relates to the crown: that area of the fontanelles which remained open to the heavens at the time of your birth, gently closing as you grounded yourself in the experience of life on earth. Violet has the capacity to reconnect you with divinity; with the gifts and purpose you have brought with you into this life. Feel the energy of the Violet as you take some deep breaths inwards towards the body. This is the Violet flame of transmutation. It is a flame that sweeps around you, burning up the dross, helping you to discover the gift within every experience of difficulty or pain. Watch it on the out-breath, as it brushes and softens the outside of your body, smoothing out the wrinkles in the aura.

Violet is the balance of heaven and earth; the harmony of masculine and feminine. As you breathe in and see this Violet light filling your crown and moving downwards through your body, notice how you begin to feel full and strong. Violet is the link with other realms, where all things are before they are born and after they return to spirit. In this dimension, surrounded and suffused by Violet light, you can leave stresses and burdens behind. You can float, light and free. Feel the gentleness of the Violet ray as it surrounds you. Feel the love, the support of all the spirit beings around you: those who may be known, unknown, or yet to be known. This is a ray of maturity and completion. Receive the Violet and accept its healing nourishment, which regenerates the body as it refreshes the mind. Take the Violet light to areas of pain, allowing it to wash through them, bringing soothing balm, relieving distress.

Continue to breathe Violet, in and out, until your whole being feels harmonised and restored. When your need for this ray is satisfied, allow the Violet light to dissipate gently into the clear light of the atmosphere around you, make a firm connection with the earth below, and when you feel ready, open your eyes.

MAGENTA

Magenta is a ray which soothes or stimulates according to the need. As you breathe in this colour, feel the richness of its energy. It brings you the warmth and gentleness of Pink, together with the power and passion of Red. Magenta hints at the transformative quality of Violet, leading you from one cycle into the next as you search to discover the job that you are here to do. If you are in need of regeneration, Magenta will restore you; if you are anxious or nervous, Magenta will calm you. Breathe this ray in deeply, and feel the need in yourself to which it will respond. Beginning above the crown, Magenta can move, with each inward breath, down the whole of your body, sinking lower, into the depths of your abdomen and right into your feet.

You are walking, now, along a quiet footpath. Magenta-coloured autumn fruits surround you: blackberries and plums, blueberries and black cherries. There is a fullness in the harvest which everywhere offers you sustenance. You may touch this fruit; feel its texture; taste its juice. As you walk on, breathing in the Magenta with each new breath, you find that the path leads to an arbour of trees. Enter into this arbour. The ground beneath your feet is soft; the sky above is clear; all around you is a perfect circle of trees which are still thick with leaves. Here you can create whatever you choose: a room; a garden; whatever space you wish to have for times of quiet contemplation. The Magenta ray connects you with the energy of absolute love. Create within this Magenta arbour a space which feeds and nurtures you in every way that you can be cherished. Bask in the Magenta which permeates the atmosphere. Bring into it flowers and music; sounds and smells. Share this space with a person or people you love, or keep it for your own use, undisturbed.

Stay within this Magenta place for as long as you wish, drinking in the colour that surrounds you there. Know that this Magenta haven is one where you can return in your imagination at any time that you may feel depleted, drained of the energy expended in caring for those around you. Feel the regeneration in your body and soul, as the Magenta washes through you and refills empty places. When you feel that, for the moment, your Magenta needs are met, take a few deep breaths and bring your attention into the present moment, to the floor beneath you, to the sounds around you. Allow the Magenta to return to its source, and when you feel ready, open your eyes.

WHITE

It is a bright, shining day in midwinter. Everything is covered in soft fresh snow. The sun, gleaming in a clear sky, sends its rays to wink and glitter on the Whiteness of the ground; of the rooftops; of the trees. Covered head-to-toe in a warm White fleece, you are walking comfortably in this silvery landscape. The cool air is exhilarating and refreshing. All around you is the full spectrum of White light, sharpening all that you see. Breathe the clear White light deep into your lungs, noticing as its biting coldness turns rapidly to inner warmth and, with each inward breath, a new vitality. As you breathe out, feel the deep cleansing as the breath carries away with it the anxieties, stresses and any other negativity which has obstructed the clarity of your perception. With each outward breath you feel cleaner and clearer; every inward breath brings you a new offering of vitality and strength. Feel the White light; fill your heart and lungs. Feel as it moves deeper, bringing light to the very centre of your being, expanding to flood gently into every cell. Watch the cells of your body soften and relax, as the fluid Whiteness streams into them, glistening, cleansing, uplifting.

You are walking gently uphill now, higher and higher. Hills turn almost to mountains, and each new step brings a wider view. After a while, you find yourself at the very top of the highest spot. The landscape, iced like fairyland, is spread out below and all around you. Situations and people in your life take on a distance, and also a new clarity. Breathing in the pure White light here on the hilltop, you can be fully and completely in the present. Allow pains, angers and sorrows to waft away; and make space for the invigorating, purifying quality of this White light that will wash and renew you.

Stay in this place for as long as you need to. When you feel replete with the Whiteness and cleanliness of the light, take a few more deep breaths, noticing the new purity of the out-breath as well as that which moves in, and then – in your own time – open your eyes.

Further Information

Philippa Merivale is an international teacher, broadcaster and counsellor in colour therapy with many years of experience in the UK, Far East, Europe and the Americas. She is the author of *Healing with Colour*, published in 1998 by Element Books; and of *The Pocket Book of Colour Power*, published by Laramar (available Summer 2000).

Seminars

In addition to writing and broadcasting, Philippa Merivale runs occasional *"Colour Talks!"* workshops based on the ideas presented in this book. She is also available, by invitation and on an occasional basis, to facilitate seminars abroad. For details please refer to our website below.

Colour Products and Forthcoming Publications

For information about forthcoming publications, and colour consultations or colour products, please visit our website: **www.colourup.co.uk**

We hope you have enjoyed this book; and we should be happy to receive any of your feedback, stories or suggestions in relation to it. You may e-mail us via the website above, or at: **merivale@globalnet.co.uk**

Further Reading

Healing with Colour: An Experience of Aura-Soma, Philippa Merivale, Element Books 1998.
Healing with Colour, Helen Graham, Gill & Macmillan 1996.
The Miracle of Colour Healing, Vicky Wall, Thorsons 1993.
Colour Me Healing, Jack Allanach, Element Books 1998.
Colour Energy, Inger Naess, Colour Energy Corporation 1996.
The Light Medicine of the Future, Jacob Lieberman.
Aura-Soma: Healing through Color, Plant, and Crystal Energy, Irene Dalichow and Mike Booth, Hay House 1996.
Understanding Auras, Joseph Ostrom, Thorsons 1993.
Auras: An Essay on the Meaning of Colors, Edgar Cayce, A.R.E. Press, 1945, 1973.
Tantra: The Art of Conscious Loving, Charles & Caroline Muir, Mercury House 1989.
Men are from Mars, Women are from Venus, John Gray, Thorsons 1993.
Create Your Own Love Story, David W. McMillan, Beyond Words Publishing 1997.
Journey of the Heart, John Welwood, Thorsons 1995.
Love and Awakening, John Welwood, Harper Perennial 1997.
Creating Affluence, Deepak Chopra, Bantam Press 1999.
The Seven Spiritual Laws of Success, Deepak Chopra, Bantam Press 1996.
The Road Less Travelled, M. Scott Peck, Arrow 1990.
People of the Lie, M. Scott Peck, Arrow 1990.
Conversations with God, Neale Donald Walsch, Hodder & Stoughton 1995.
Awaken the Giant Within, Anthony Robbins, Simon & Schuster 1992.
The Celestine Prophecy, James Redfield, Warner Books 1993.

Acknowledgments

Relationship is a pretty wide-ranging subject in anyone's life; so there are many more people I should like to thank than can be mentioned individually here: family members, friends and colleagues, past and present.

There are a few people, or groups, who must nevertheless be given special mention: My parents, Norah and Stephen Merivale. Roger and Anne Ormrod, for setting the precedent, and for never giving up on me. Noelle Zaradin, for perpetual generosity and love. Aura-Soma, for a basic tool kit, and the freedom to develop it in my own way. Jamie Mackay, for Dutch courage and a safe roof. Michael Skipwith, for health, wisdom and common sense. Patricia Merivale, for everything. Aunt Rosemary, for staying until she did. William Grey-Campbell, for constancy, clear sight and sanity. Rania Schachter, for vital editorial criticism, generosity and encouragement, as well as ongoing friendship and inspiration. Lynn Robinson, for great editorial input, spot-on timing and the clarity to stay with the vision. Susan and Hugh Hamilton, for blowing up the ball at the beginning. Sachiko Noda, for getting the ball rolling. Susan Tillett, for the initiative to act, and Diantha Harris for joining in. Ellen Epstein, for keeping the ball rolling, and later for editorial help and enthusiasm. Elaine Horton, for companionship, guidance and helpful reading. Tiffany Windsor, for flying in at the most appropriate moment. All my students and all my clients, for teaching me most of what I have learned.

Many unmet authors, and a few songwriters, who have been my roadside companions on a long journey (and I offer my apologies to those few I have quoted without permission or source references, in the cases when I have lost these — I will endeavour to put this right before reprinting).

Lastly, but above all, my immediate family. These include John — my consort, my fiercest critic (especially in the writing of this book), and my best friend — and my children Nicola, Stephen and Magdalen. They have all given me love, without conditions, in conditions that were sometimes indescribable.

Index

QUICK ORDERS

Telephone orders

Call 0870 241 2850

Have your credit card ready.

Website orders

www.colourup.co.uk

Item	Price	Quantity	Total
1) *Colour Talks!* – Book	£11.99		£
2) *Colour Talks!* – CD Colour Visualisations	£10.99 (Inc. VAT)		£

Please add despatch payment:
UK, Eire and Channel Islands.*

Order value		please add	
up to	£12.00	£1.95	£
between	£12.01 and £25	£2.95	£
between	£25.01 and £35	15%	£
between	£35.01 and £100	10%	£
over	£100.01	5%	£

Total order value   **£**

*Overseas orders: please phone for advice